YOU ONLY GET ONE LIFE
BRIGITTE NIELSEN

YOU ONLY GET ONE LIFE

BRIGITTE NIELSEN

JOHN BLAKE

Published by John Blake Publishing Ltd,
3 Bramber Court, 2 Bramber Road,
London W14 9PB, England

www.johnblakepublishing.co.uk

www.facebook.com/Johnblakepub facebook
twitter.com/johnblakepub twitter

First published in hardback in 2011

ISBN: 978-1-84358-342-4

British Library Cataloguing-in-Publication Data:

A catalogue record for this book is available from the British Library.

Design by www.envydesign.co.uk

Printed in Great Britain by CPI Mackays, Chatham, ME5 8TD

1 3 5 7 9 10 8 6 4 2

God, grant me the serenity
To accept the things I cannot change;
Courage to change the things I can;
And wisdom to know the difference.

With thanks to Peter Bennett for his
professional support.

Thanks to Brunina, Eva and Caroline,
my best girlfriends.

CONTENTS

PROLOGUE

You've probably seen me in movies or on TV, or read about me in the media. Never mind a book – you could fill an entire library with what other people have said about me. And when I was young, I used to follow it all. I loved it when I read the good stuff but the criticism always got to me so in the end I decided to live my life to the full and not worry about what anyone else thought.

It's been an incredible ride for someone like me who started off as a little girl in an unremarkable suburb of north Copenhagen. It's been hectic and full of wonderful experiences but like anyone else I have also had my share of surprises. We all know those moments... when things change and your life takes an unexpected turn. It might be sickness or the loss of loved ones or it could be something amazingly good.

The defining moment in my life came on an afternoon in 1978 when a woman I had never met before tapped me on the shoulder in the street and introduced me to a glamorous existence I could barely have imagined, let alone dream I might inhabit. Me, a skinny, freakishly tall outcast of a teenager – but I became an overnight sensation: a supermodel living out the red carpet dream. I grew up and have lived the rest of my life in public – whether or not I have wanted to have everything on display. That's just the way it is when the cameras roll: you just have to be there. And that's how it was for me as the entertainer, the diva, the blonde – Brigitte with the long legs and the big breasts. She was an overnight success and a completely different person from who I used to be – shy, insecure, gawky Gitte from Rødovre in Denmark. It seemed like a fairy tale when I was chosen and I was just too young to know that there was always going to be a price to pay.

Everyone talked about my jet-set lifestyle and a string of very public relationships but with each lurid headline, I became more lonely – I didn't recognise the person I read about. I compromised who I really was with make-up, a big, open Danish smile and designer clothes. Today I know that I gave away too much of myself to pay for my travels in a world where the men and the media could never have enough from me. I cared so much about their opinions. There were too many occasions when I was not faithful to my true nature and times when I was cheated by those closest to me. In the end, it almost cost me my life.

On my 40th birthday I saw it all so clearly: my existence was no longer bearable. My bubbly, energetic and trusting soul had been all but wiped out, but although there seemed to be only one way out for me at the time I realise now that those experiences, good and bad, have made me who I am today – Gitte Nielsen, not Brigitte. In other words, the person I always used to be happy about being and who I am once again unconditionally proud to be.

I don't know why so many long years had to pass before I finally accepted myself for who I am, rather than seeing myself as the world saw me, but these days I've definitely got my priorities right: first a mother, then a wife and then comes work. I still give my best, but I know what's more important.

When I finally decided to tell my story, I knew I would have to open my heart and show the whole world who Gitte Nielsen really is – and she's very different from the confident sex symbol given the name 'Brigitte' by a Hollywood movie mogul who decided that 'Gitte' didn't work in films. Gitte didn't sound like a star, people wouldn't even know the Danish way of saying it – '*Ghee-tah*' – and she has been lost inside Brigitte for too long. Being Gitte always seemed safe, whereas Brigitte was the dangerous, exciting one. Being Brigitte was the cause of all my trouble.

My friends told me I should let everyone know what I am really like, and it's not what you read in the gossip pages. My story, what really happened to me, could have happened to anyone: we all row the same boat. You may even recognise yourself in me. And you may see your story in my adventures – after all, we Danes know all about fairy tales! Hans Christian Andersen wrote some of the best; remember the ugly duckling who grew into the beautiful, long-necked swan? But the Danes also gave the world the Viking – the most feared warrior of them all – even if it was the Victorians who invented the detail of the horned helmet. You'll find me somewhere between those three points – warrior, graceful swan and, paddling hard to keep up, the ugly duckling, dreaming of being accepted, happy and loved.

I had two cousins who always had long blonde hair and blue eyes, while I was stuck with light brown hair and an endless parade of cold-sores on my lips. My grandmother was the only one who saw anything in the way I looked. She would take my face in her cool hands and smooth my hair back gently. 'Look at this elegant forehead,' she whispered to me. 'You're going to be beautiful.'

Tell my classmates that. I was bullied mercilessly for my height and my skinniness. I changed schools seven times and I was always very lonely. My academic record was great but I was always the last to be picked for any games and unlike the other girls, I never got love letters. You never forget those years. When I became successful it was the turn of the press to keep me under pressure: they wanted to know every detail about my relationships with the brutal guys I frequently seemed to end up with. It hurt me just as much as any of the taunts at school.

You have to fight for your own happiness, that's what I know now. You're the only one in charge of your life. Happiness won't come easily and you really have to think hard about how you do things.

I think my story will move a lot of people. Some people will be surprised, and others will be upset. Some will ask, 'Who does she think she is?' But that's how it is when you tell the truth. The only person I know for sure will be proud is my dad. He died when he was very young and when he looks down, he'll smile – and I'll be smiling back. Dad knew the truth can hurt but that you have to face things without flinching. I'm not really religious myself, except in as much as I believe there is a god who lives on in all of us – that is the divine in everyone, a force for good.

Looking back on my first 47 years I think of the Danish girl who grew up in the west side of '60s Copenhagen. She was a powerful thing with an appetite for life and she went looking for experiences that most girls would never even dream of. As Brigitte, life has been fun and fantastic, and I took a lot of chances along the way – probably more than I should have. Mostly, I got away with it pretty much unscathed. I'd always leap into the unknown, dive headlong into swimming pools in my life without checking if there was water in them first. Even though I don't believe in an actual god, somebody somewhere was watching me. I got away with doing things that, by rights, should have killed me.

I'd like to thank everyone who has been involved in this book and who has helped me. Most of all my fantastic father and Mattia Dessi, my husband, who saved me from the bottle and is the reason why today I am clear and full of energy. And of course my kids, Julian, Killian, Douglas and Raoulino. I love you so much.

Gitte Nielsen
London, May 2011

CHAPTER 1

GOODBYE

Life is leaving me. Slowly... and I can feel it happening. Second by second. The weeks and the months that became years of pain are washing over me and I'm sinking into darkness. I can still make out the walls of my bathroom as I lie on the floor. I'm in the villa on Lake Lugano where I've lived for 12 years, but it doesn't feel real.

The room is big, but somehow it now feels even bigger, as if everything is receding. It's going away and I don't care, though once it meant so much to me. We built it ourselves: we put our love and a whole lot of money and sweat into making it a dream home. I try to move, fall heavily back on the floor but don't notice the pain. This bathroom, like everywhere else in the villa, is light, airy and finished in a grand style. It all looked so elegant, so perfect. This house was going to be our refuge. Now it's all shaky and hard to make out, a badly-tuned television picture.

The sun streams through the window and even though I can't feel its warmth, I'm feeling good. I'm wrapped up in cotton wool of my own making. I feel safe. The radio next door drifts through and it sounds distorted, like hearing music underwater. When I was in the bath as a kid I would dunk my head and feel the warmth of the water and a peaceful sensation of the indistinct sounds of the world elsewhere.

I can make out the melody. Celine Dion is singing 'A New Day Has Come'. I've met her many times, and I think about her beauty and that instantly recognisable voice. My own career in music never really took off... now it's too late. It's strange how clear my mind is. I'm a bird, no longer frantically flapping but gliding in effortless swoops. I register my senses, the smell of the day's many cigarettes, the sour, lingering taste of the bottle of Jack Daniel's which lies empty on its side by the sink. My breath stinks.

How long have I been here now? I can't tell by the sun whether it's still morning or afternoon yet. Actually, I don't know what day it is. It's probably school time, I decide, because I can't hear the kids. Where's my husband Raoul? I don't know. I honestly don't care. It won't be long now.

Two floors down, the cook is preparing something. The sound of the gardener drifts in with birdsong through the open window. We live just outside a village and I think I can also hear the sound of its church bells. Next to me on the floor is the glass which I filled with pills. There were about 25 of them. I swallowed them one at a time and now there's about five left. The last six or seven were tough; I had to use water to knock them back. They were strong painkillers prescribed for my back pain – with the same effect as Valium.

I'd had the pills for a long time. My left leg is five centimetres longer than the right. As a young girl I'd been diagnosed with scoliosis, which made my spine into an S-shape. I had to wear a medical corset for two years. Every so often I would be almost paralysed with pain and breathing itself became an effort. It felt as if the nerve endings in my back were exposed and someone was grabbing at them. I always had those strong painkillers around for when things got really bad and over the years I'd learned to manage the condition. Now the same pills are going to be used to end my psychological pain.

I think about how the world keeps turning and life in the beautiful surroundings of the lake goes on. All the passion I had for making this place my home has drained away, but I stayed because of the pact I made with myself. I told myself there would be no packing my bags just because things got difficult: I was going to stick it out and have order and stability in my marriage just like my parents had. I'd been determined that I was going to be with my husband until we grew old together. We were going to raise our family here. And I had been very happy to begin with, but what was going to be my own version of paradise had slowly, stealthily, turned into a prison. Everything I once loved, I now hated.

One of the first to discover the charms of Lugano was Charlie Chaplin. Singer Robert Palmer lived and died here. Stravinsky and Tchaikovsky composed on its shores in the shadows of the Alps. It's almost too pretty, a chocolate-box scene that could seduce anyone.

Our house had been owned by a Swiss baron who was

ruined in the casinos back in the 1920s. The building fell into decay until Raoul and I fell in love with it and set to work. We were on the border with Italy where I was doing a lot of TV work. Switzerland was popular with high earners – and it was where Raoul came from. He had to return home and Lugano seemed like a good place to start our life as a married couple. The paparazzi never made it out there and I could escape the stress of my high-maintenance lifestyle. We were secure. You could wander around completely naked if you wanted. Here I could live out my dream of being a normal wife and mother with an ordinary family: I would be Gitte at last.

It wasn't to be. I should have listened to the voice inside me which was screaming for me to grab the kids and get out of there, but I was determined to make it work and I used everything, all my money, all my energy. Now I had nothing left and I realised that there was no other way out.

I thought our marriage was exactly what I needed, but we haven't had sex for more than two years. We've all heard about cults that brainwash people into doing things they wouldn't normally do. I didn't believe that really happened, but now I understand. I can't bear what I have become and I no longer recognise myself: when I look in the mirror I don't see smart, strong, independent Gitte. Where is she? I don't have the strength any more – I'm broken. Just tell me what to do and I'll do it. I'm on a treadmill fuelled by alcohol – that's all there is in my life now.

Now I'm sure of what I want: I know I'm doing the right thing. It doesn't seem selfish to me and I'm not thinking about the kids. Everything makes sense. I haven't got the resources to plan so there won't be anything as organised as a suicide note, no instructions for my funeral service, no thought about what should happen with my remains and there's nothing significant about choosing today to die. It might just as well have been yesterday and it might have come over me tomorrow. Maybe it's the way the sun is shining through the windows this morning or the quiet drone of activity from the village or the gardener working downstairs. I'm not really sure. I just need peace: I want to smell it, taste it, feel it.

I had considered drowning myself in the lake but the thought of the ice-cold water put me off. I'd heard that death by drowning is the worst of all ways to die. The pills just make me feel light, sleepy. This is the peace I am looking for. I will drift off and never wake up again.

I'm a bit disappointed that it hasn't happened yet – I thought it would be quicker than this. But now it's coming. I feel really relaxed and I'm not at all scared. For the first time in a long time there is pain neither in my mind nor my body. I get a strange sensation, something turning in my stomach. I've cried so many tears – it feels like I've cried every day for years. I've become so used to unbearable pain that the sudden absence makes me realise how hard it has been to be me.

No more lies, no more guilt, no more feelings. The world is closing down around me and that reflection I didn't recognise in the mirror is disappearing as well. I'm smiling, smiling, backing out of the picture. My last thought is of Marilyn Monroe and how she took an overdose. I've fallen over again but I don't feel it.

CHAPTER 2

COPENHAGEN TO CATWALK

I come from a very small suburb to the north-west of Copenhagen called Rødovre. Pretty middle class but not exactly glamorous. There's a lake there and if you were Danish, you might pay it a visit on a day out.

My destiny in life was to be a librarian like my mother or maybe a shop assistant. I had a job in a bakery and I wouldn't have minded staying. I'd have been content to save up for my yearly package holiday and I doubt I'd have dreamed of anything more ambitious than a slightly bigger house or a better car. Everyone would know me for being reliable at work and a good mother to my 2.4 children. The kids would have been good at sports and they'd have had a talent for music which might get them onto *X Factor*. They'd be popular, the neighbours would remark on how well-behaved they were, they would eventually go to university and they would get good jobs themselves. My script for life wouldn't have made a blockbuster movie but that's what should have happened.

But it didn't. My story was shaped partly by luck and in large part by me. In the alternate reality, little Gitte grew up and never left Denmark and she's running around after her kids and she's perfectly satisfied. Even now I still think that I might go back and work in that library or be the neighbourhood baker.

I asked myself why things developed the way they did when I sat down to write my story: I was trying to make sense of some of my darker experiences and I thought that it could all have been so different. Then I became convinced that I didn't have so much control in what I was doing. You only have one life and it never runs as smoothly as you think it's going to. It is made up of all these different threads and they have knots which you don't even see until you step back and really take a good look at yourself. When you're in the moment you just get yourself past the knots somehow and move on to the next thing. Most of us just don't have the time to think about our motives. You simply live the life you have with all your mistakes and flashes of genius. Writing about yourself is a really weird thing to do because you get to think about it all properly for the first time.

At least I don't have any doubt about where it all began for me. I was 16 in the summer in 1978 and I was heading straight for a famous square in Copenhagen we call Gråbrødre Torv. Full of bars with music always playing, it's popular with tourists and young girls from the suburbs who are desperate for a bit of excitement in their lives. It was a Thursday and the endless playground bullying and ridicule I'd endured for so long was about to come to an end. I was going to be appreciated; I was about to become someone to look up to, whose every whim would be indulged. This would be a fairy tale. And, as in any fairy tale, there would be a huge price to pay.

I was with my girlfriend Susanne and we had spent a couple of hours looking for clothes and shoes in local shops before taking the bus into town. We were so excited. Coming from the drab end of the city, the centre of Copenhagen was always bustling and full of life. We didn't have much money to spend but we loved to window shop. Copenhagen is a very old town with beautiful churches and I liked looking at all the statues and the buildings with their characteristic copper roofs. You look up and you know you're somewhere special. My neighbourhood seemed so sad and dark by contrast. We weren't allowed out often and there was a bit of a thrill about hanging out in town – it felt illicit and very grown-up. We had on the nearest we could get to cool clothes and we knew loads of other teens would be showing off with a beer in Gråbrødre Torv.

Susanne and I always headed for a big tree in the square which was popular with young lovers. We made our way purposefully, arm-in-arm and deep in serious conversation about – what else? – boys. Our first stop was to get a beer at a bar where I was hoping to see a certain tall and blue-eyed bartender named Christian. Between us, Susanne and I had enough for one beer and two bus tickets home. It was all very silly, but it meant everything to us.

We felt at the centre of everything, surrounded as we were by busy people and traffic; it was where all the action in Copenhagen was. I blended in here. Nobody was going to laugh at me for being too tall or too skinny. I could wear whatever I wanted, I could lose myself in the crowd. People here didn't have the time to stop and be idly malicious. In Rødovre they called me a '*giraffen*' – Danish for giraffe. I was an awkward, strange creature who always felt out of place.

Copenhagen was where it all came together for me and we were having the best time. Nothing looked more sophisticated, more gorgeous than the square. Apart from Christian. I smiled at him and when he came over to serve us I melted, grinning like an idiot. I was quickly dizzy from my half-a-beer and I didn't even like the taste of it, but I felt older and it helped my self-esteem. Drinking beer felt like the sort of thing that Christian would approve of and my heart beat faster every time he looked my way.

I made the most of my freedom. It was almost 5 o'clock and I would have to be home by 6. This was my father's deadline and there was no excuse for missing it. He was unbelievably strict. I would have to be at the dinner table and sitting up straight. Properly straight – Dad had taught me and my brother by making the pair of us sit still with a book on our heads. He had some old-fashioned ideas about parenting and I'm sure he didn't intend the advantage his lessons gave when I started modelling. While the other girls would be learning how to walk neatly down the runway, I was already on lesson two. Dad's rules at mealtimes extended to ensuring that our elbows were always down and we used knives and forks with equal elegance. That was just Dad's way.

Five o'clock and my fairy tale, as usual, was going the way of *Cinderella*. I was young and excited and in love with the world but I knew I had to get home before my dad turned me into a pumpkin. As much as I loved him, I was afraid as well and I would never have dared to cross him. All talk of boys and dreams about Christian fled from my mind as I prepared to head home. The party was over.

Susanne knew the score and we set off in plenty of time. It was always the same...until someone prodded me forcefully in the side. That had never happened before. I looked around sharply to see who was being so rude and what they wanted.

'Would you like to be a model?'

CHAPTER 3

THE HOMING PIGEON WHO DIDN'T COME BACK

I was born on 15 July 1963 to Hanne and Svend Nielsen. Back then, the Danish state provided a lot of help for newlyweds. They would automatically be offered an apartment if they were expecting a child. Our family was assigned a home in Rødovre.

Mum had a very easy pregnancy but my actual birth was horrendous for her. They ended up having to yank me out with forceps after she had battled for a couple of days to get me out on her own. I was just over 3kg and 50cm tall at birth, with blue eyes and black hair. I was an active baby, though with my round face and baby fat there was no sign that I would grow up to be 190cm tall.

After a year we moved to a nondescript two-storey house that was a popular style at the time. It had the red bricks that marked '50s construction in Denmark and it consisted of a long narrow kitchen, two small rooms for us kids and another bedroom for my parents. There was also an Lshaped living room and a terrace. Outside was a little shed.

When I got a brother, Jan, soon after our little family unit was complete. Jan and I were very close. We had to be – I didn't have many friends and Dad's strict rules meant we were rarely allowed out to play with other kids. Dad had some very weird ways. We would always have to clean the house after school, unlike most of the other kids. Danish society has a reputation for being laidback but you wouldn't have thought it, had you seen the Nielsen household.

Jan and I would entertain ourselves by playing cards or having fun out in the garden, finding amusing things to do or playing football together. We had a cocker spaniel which we'd take out for walks and we both liked to cycle. I was very protective of my little brother and always made sure that nobody hurt him – apart from me. Whenever we fought he'd invariably get a big-sisterly beating from me. I was terrible! He used to irritate me but at the same time we were a team. You'd never have got between us at school or in the neighbourhood streets, but at home whenever one of us did something wrong, we'd always blame the other. Quite a lot of the time we'd confuse our parents so much that they quite forgot about punishing us – either that or they'd punish us both. At least then we weren't suffering alone. I was often the one who would lead us into adventure and mischief then and although these days we don't see each other so much, we still feel as connected. He's a successful businessman based in Denmark and he travels a lot, but we're soul mates and when we get back together, we fool around as if we were still kids.

My room was on the first floor backing onto the garden. I was miserable most of the time and it was there that I gazed out over the middle-class neighbourhood. The gardens were always well-maintained and as it rains in Denmark almost as much as it does in the UK, they were always green. The really smart homes would have a flagpole planted in their gardens. Strange, huh? If you had a flag in your garden it meant you thought you were a slightly better class of person – that's just a very Danish thing! I would stare into the distance, past the flags and the neat little patches of grass, and I daydreamed my childhood away.

We were seven kilometres from Rådhuspladsen, the centre of Copenhagen and the square at the heart of the business district. It might as well have been seven light years. We were much closer to the Damhussøen lake. That was my escape from the identikit houses that looked as if they were out of some science-fiction nightmare where everyone was the same. The lake was where I got away from our strict house rules and my unhappiness with my physical appearance.

My grandmother lived in a house just by the lake. It was magical for a little kid. Whenever I could, I would take my bike and cycle as fast as I could to see her. She was on the far side and I would have to go all the way around. There was a little fun park near the lake and I always stopped at an aviary where they had homing pigeons. In a tradition dating back years, the birds were released each week and my dad explained that some of them would fly some 500 kilometres to get back home. They had probably once served an important purpose for the town but now it was just done for the sport. None of that mattered to me – I was just amazed by their bravery. Imagine being hundreds of kilometres from everything you knew and having to find your way back! It was so romantic for me as a child who was often sickly. When the birds were due back I would speed down on my bike and stare hard, heart pounding, as tiny black dots against the expanse of sky resolved themselves into the familiar shapes of those bold scouts making their return. They'd always come back with messages. I imagined they would be bringing fantastic stories of faraway lands where daily life wasn't measured by the size of your flagpole or the shape of one's lawn.

'I wish they could talk,' I'd say.

I wondered about the men who sent them off and what they thought. I'd hear the wings flutter when they were readied for release and hear the excited noises from the birds. When they circled ready to make their journey I wanted to clap, jump and shout encouragement – but I was always too shy.

My own attempts to make a break for it were rather less successful. I started early, when I was just three. Liselotte was my best friend and she came from a wealthy middle-class family, with a father who was a dentist. She was the opposite of me, small and quiet while I was the tomboy. Liselotte was a year older but it was me who convinced her to go on an adventure with our tricycles. 'We'll go and see my grandmother,' I told her and we set off to find the lake.

I have no idea how we got away with it, but we did, and Grandma gave us juice and cake. I savoured every mouthful, all the while knowing that I was going to be in big trouble with my parents who were already on their way to pick us up. I got a smack off my dad but it didn't put me off adventuring. Liselotte and I stayed friends for years and I was always hungry for excitement. I liked nothing better than to pack a bag with some supplies and head off into the unknown with my trusty bike. One time we somehow managed to find our way onto a motorway. The police found us and there was definitely no cake. I was always the one who was being reckless. The result was another smack and one week grounded.

When I was on my own I often cycled about five kilometres to Heden, a beautiful open space, flat and tranquil. I got off my bike and lay on the grass, gazing into the white clouds and daydreamed. One day a handsome man would ride up on his horse and take me away from all the bad things to a magic land. Rødovre was safe, it was all right, but I was never comfortable. Something about the place didn't agree with me. *L202, 212*

For a start, I was always sick. As a baby I had streptococcal blood disorder which affected me for a long time around the age of two. My hair fell out and I had a very high fever. I was in and out of hospital for months while the doctors tried to find out what was wrong with me. Three years passed and they prescribed so much medication that I had to go to a specialist hospital reserved for children so sick that they can't live normally. I was five, but I was still the size of a two-year-old and very thin. 'Will I be like this forever?' I asked. It was a pretty big question for a five-year-old.

I later discovered myself as a mother of four that kids are amazingly resilient. They can survive the most devastating illnesses and I did get better. I didn't even remember much about the sickness myself. It was very different for my parents, who found it unbearable to watch their child suffer. They felt completely helpless that whatever they tried to do didn't work. I realised just how bad it must have been when my youngest son Raoulino was diagnosed with a non-cancerous brain tumour at the age of eight. As it grew he was at risk from bleeding in the brain and he was sick for two years. He's fine now, but at the time they told us he could die at any moment. I felt that gnawing terror that my parents felt at an illness which doesn't seem to have a cure.

My own memories of being a very young child were happy ones. The best times were when our yearly holiday took us to Orø. We never had the money to go on foreign holidays and instead we went to this tiny island north of Copenhagen. We piled into the old, embarrassing car with all the luggage tied on top with a rope; at least my parents allowed me to take Liselotte with us.

The holiday home was old and little more than a not particularly large, wooden box. One room included the kitchen with its single-ring stove while the toilet was outside with a hole, but it made for the most memorable vacation even if you'd swear our cramped quarters could never hold all of us. It didn't matter though, because for once the rules were relaxed and that was enough to make it paradise.

I was allowed to hide, to run around and – my favourite thing – to climb trees. As a kid, I was like a monkey and I would lose myself for whole days at a time and could be as dangerous as I liked. The island was only about 14 kilometres in total, small enough for the adults to be reassured that we were probably safe but large enough for it to be an exciting wilderness for us. It was warm and I was surrounded by the people I trusted the most. Mum and Dad were relaxed and in a good mood and nothing could hurt us. We'd head off with backpacks stuffed with food and drink. Liselotte was by my side just as she'd always been since we were little.

We went down to the water to laugh at birdwatchers. All were totally absorbed in what they were doing, some motionless, gazing straight up with their noses in the air while others stared intently for minutes at a time, seemingly at a patch of sand. They had no idea that they were providing the cabaret: they were hilarious in their seriousness and the way they seemed completely oblivious to anything if it didn't have feathers or live in an egg. You could get right up close to them and they wouldn't react at all. Then we ran off to throw ourselves in the sand dunes and look for seals in the water.

That holiday was also the first time I fell in love. Vesti was the son of the shopkeeper who ran the island's tiny supermarket. He had dark, curly hair and dark eyes and I remember their long, dark eyelashes, they were so beautiful. And he made me laugh. I dreamed about him the whole summer.

I was only nine years old but I can still remember the way he smelled and a wonderful feeling of tingly excitement, like I had something sparkling and fizzy in my stomach, every time I looked at him. It was a confusing sensation that I first got to know in the shower when I was eight.

I'd spilled marmalade all over my clothes and my mother got me to take off the sticky things and clean myself up. I never needed any encouragement to get in the water and I loved to bathe – I was a real waterbaby. My hair was washed in the shower and I got soap all over myself. I directed the showerhead all over my body and when the jet played between my legs, I felt this jolt of excitement.

I had no idea what I'd discovered with my showerhead, but I liked it. The warm sensation was strong and tickly all over my body if I kept the showerhead in a particular position and whatever it was, it felt fantastic. After a while it would get to be almost too nice. I had to change position occasionally otherwise it felt like I might go crazy – but I always brought it back again. How long was I doing it for – five minutes? Ten? I don't know; I lost all sense of time.

The experience opened a door to a completely new world and I was eager to understand what it was all about. In some ways I was already an experienced young lady by the time I got to meet Vesti: I had already met the feeling that he aroused in me and I knew myself quite well by then. The physical world I was exploring and the world of love came together in Vesti. At the time, I just wasn't old enough to make a conscious connection between the two. I couldn't quite work out what the difference was between the love I felt with my trusty showerhead and the love in the presence of Vesti. The best I could work it out was that the feeling I got in the shower would always end quite abruptly. When it was over – it was over. What I felt around Vesti lingered on. I was to spend many years later on trying to bring the two worlds of the physical and the emotional together.

The love I found on holiday was new. It was warm,

exciting and it was a comforting sensation. I felt safe, although I know many women wouldn't compare love to safety. For me it was everything. And of course that kind of love only works when the other person feels that safety too and you get the feeling returned. Vesti seemed interested to me but I'm now sure that it was basically just me who was in love. We were, after all, only nine and I don't think he had much to return to me. I was just ecstatic to have those feelings – I felt so proud, so grown-up. This was the thing that meant the most to me in my life – and it has done ever since then.

Love has come and gone over the years, but I would never have wanted to have lived without those sensations, no matter how hard it's got at times. Maybe Vesti was something of a red flag if only I'd been old enough to understand it. Love requires all the energy I have in my body and soul. Even at nine it demanded everything of me and I felt that slight edge of madness that comes with it. I think I was even then somewhat addicted to that tremendous kick. That was an indication of a less healthy side of love. But if Vesti had been a warning of what was to come, do I regret ignoring it? No. I wouldn't have missed out on any of my adventures in love. They took me to surprising places and even if they were on occasion places I wouldn't want to go, that's just the way it was: you can't control where love takes you.

I never got to hold Vesti's hand and we never kissed. He probably just thought I was stupid for being so interested in him. But in our eight- and nine-year-old ways we expressed our feelings. He chased me, we'd tease each other and hang out. We were just doing normal kid stuff but holding Vesti's attention was what gave me that special tingly sensation.

The other love that started that summer would prove to be life-long. Liselotte and I found a farm with a couple of ponies, which the owners allowed us to ride. I was instantly smitten and fell for a pony called Magic. I don't know what kind he was or how old, but I wanted to be with him as much as possible. I looked after him, fed him and would take him out for rides. Sometimes I would just push my face into the warmth of his mane – I loved the intoxicating smell of horses all over me. I've been mad about riding ever since. Everything about horses is wonderful – hugging them, taking them out to gallop over the hills or just listening to them after a ride in the evening when they're chomping feed in the stables.

Riding the ponies that summer made me feel so serene. When we got back from holiday I would cycle to stables outside Copenhagen every day and spend hours grooming horses. In return I got an hour of free riding every week. I gazed into those big, dark eyes that were large enough to absorb all my thoughts and I'd feel them take away the meanness of ordinary life. The relationship with them was easy and honest. Riding can be as technically demanding as you want to make it, but it all comes down to moving each part of your body to the rhythm and motion of the horse. It wasn't so much a sport as a way of becoming one with this beautiful animal.

I didn't stop my regular rides until I became a model – and it came in useful later when I got the lead in *Red Sonja* opposite Arnold Schwarzenegger. We had to do so much on horseback that I'd never have been able to do it without all my experience. I took it up again when I got married to Sylvester Stallone and we took up indoor polo with other Hollywood horse fanatics. Later, when I was in a relationship with American footballer Mark Gastineau, I had my own horse again. Mark was born and grew up on a ranch and he was always around horses. I learned how to ride bareback, on Western saddle, and I got to try roping. I don't have so much time to fit in riding these days but it's still a form of therapy for me, like some people go for a walk or cook a meal. I like to be close to the horse; feeling its calming heartbeat always makes me happier – it's got to be only a matter of time before I get my own horse once more. I'll never give it up. I'd love to live the rural life with Mattia, owning chickens, pigs and a pony somewhere outside London – there's nothing like the smell of the hay and the nuzzle of an affectionate horse.

CHAPTER 4

A GIRAFFE IN DESIGNER CLOTHES

My first thought: this woman must mean Susanne. She's pushed me, but there's no way I could be a model. You know when you see two girls out together and one is always good-looking and the other one is ugly? Those were basically the roles Susanne and I played. I was the beautiful girl's friend and it had always worked perfectly well. It wasn't like I thought it was going to be any other way. Almost as a reflex I stepped out of the way so that Susanne could talk to the woman who had stopped us.

She looked to be about 30 and she was still smiling. 'No, no, it's *you* I'm talking to,' she said, looking directly at me. 'My name is Marianne Diers and I'm a talent scout for Copenhagen Models and Elite. Would you like to be a model?'

It was a simple enough question, but first let me tell you a little bit about me and my body. We'd never got on very well together. I hated the way I looked and I would do everything I could not to be seen. The opinion seemed to be shared by most of the kids I knew. I studied hard at school because I was sure I would only be able to rely on what was inside me to get me through life. The taunts of *giraffen* really stung, but I also believed them: it was as if it was my fault that I was such a tall thing. By the age of 11, I was taller than my own teacher and in an attempt to disguise it, I would deliberately stoop slightly so as not to be noticed.

It was around this time that my parents noticed my spine had gone crooked with what was diagnosed as scoliosis. The doctors pointed out then that one leg was shorter than the other. This condition is painful and if it's not treated properly in children then it can cause problems into adult life. I wore a medical corset for more than a year, but that was okay because I could wear it under my regular clothes.

But the doctors also said I had to wear special orthopaedic shoes to compensate for the difference in the length of my legs and at that point I rebelled. I wore those hateful shoes for two days and never put them on again. Already I had the corset, braces and I was stooped over with my height – I felt like some kind of freak. I had to go to physiotherapy every Friday until at last the doctors decided they weren't getting the results they needed: they wanted to remove a piece of my knee, warning that the procedure carried a 50 per cent chance of leaving me with a permanently stiff leg. Thank God my dad told them the operation was completely out of the question: we would carry on working on the condition but my parents wouldn't run the risk of me being permanently damaged.

There was also trouble in my mouth: I wore braces and the dentist had to take out six of my teeth. You could park bicycles in the gaps, it was a nightmare! Now I couldn't even smile as I dragged my extra-long leg around and tried to avoid banging my head on the ceiling. It was not a good scene and all of this was going on at the same time, so I felt really unlucky.

I compensated by working very hard and got myself a job in the local library in an effort to feel there was something I could do to make up for the way I looked. I had the best grades and I got two 13s – you could only get that if you were as good as your teacher. I was so happy with that. When my German teacher asked for a volunteer to learn all the irregular verbs, I put up my hand and said I'd do it over the weekend. There were more than 200 of them and the teacher thought it would be impossible. I said I'd do it if he bought ice cream for everyone on Monday. I did nothing else but study that weekend and when we got back, I had them all down perfectly. Everyone cheered me for the first time: 'Gitte got us ice cream!' And I felt so happy and proud – it was one of the best days I ever had at school.

Mostly I would feel a terrible knot in my stomach that tightened whenever it was break time. I was always alone in the playground and the other kids were often having a laugh at my expense. As I write about my schooldays now I get that same sick feeling of dread just remembering how horrible it was: it was the worst kind of pain. Even my medical conditions weren't as bad as knowing that I was an outcast. Girls passed around invitations to birthday parties and they always made a point of handing them to everyone around me, which made it perfectly obvious that I was excluded. It was even worse in the mornings after parties: they made sure I was in earshot when they talked about how much fun it had been, what games they played and how many presents they got. I regularly cried in the evenings before I went to bed and it was only my friendship with Liselotte and thoughts of my beloved horses that kept me sane.

I felt different and wrong for so long that my school years now seem like one great fog. The others whispered about me and even when I wasn't there, I could tell by the way that people looked at me when I came into the room that they had been talking. It was endless. The laughter rubbed me raw, along with their delight when they could tell they'd got to me. I remember running away from their malicious giggling in the playground, falling over my own gangly legs and scraping myself badly when my jeans tore at the knee. The laughter became hysteria as I picked myself up and painfully made my escape again. It was particularly hard going home in the winter: the kids would kill me with icy snowballs on the way back. They waited for me and every day it was the same shit. We all moved on to the same schools in the neighbourhood so it never got better, even as I got older.

The teachers knew what was going on. It's not like today when something like that would be treated with great seriousness. Now parents would be called in, meetings would be had. Back then, you just had to get on with it: you fall down, you stand up, you move on. We know how mean children can be, but in those days adults simply weren't interested in understanding how bad it was, they didn't listen to us.

Classes often shared the same room and I remember

coming in and moving a boy's bag to hang up my satchel on the hooks that lined the wall near my desk. He was with the class going out and saw me move his bag. 'She's going to fucking get it,' he said to his friends. My heart immediately started racing and as soon as school finished, I raced out of there as if my life depended on it – which it did. Six boys tore after me and I ended up in some apartment block banging on a stranger's door. Fortunately, I was let in by a kind lady who called my parents for me. It was a rare rescue from the regular daily beating, and it was only after that incident that I finally moved school, away from Liselotte and I had to start again.

I suffered from psychosomatic stomach pains, but when I got home I'd still eat at the appointed hour of 6 o'clock and clean up the house. 'How is everything?' my parents would ask. I'd tell them school was fine. We didn't talk much more in the home than I did with the teachers – I didn't have that kind of relationship with my parents or my grandmother. My grades were always good so they never suspected anything. Jan and I would usually have to go to our rooms after supper. We didn't have friends over and I remember having to ask my mum before she'd give me a goodnight kiss. That's just how it was in my family.

So if it was me who was being asked to be a model there had to be a catch. I thought I'd have to strip or be in some kind of pornographic magazine. 'I'll have to ask my dad first,' I told her and that became my standard response to any offer of work until the day he died. It made me feel safe. Besides, I did want time to check it out. I didn't want to give the other kids at school a fresh chance to laugh at me if it turned out to be bullshit. Having been called ugly and stupid for so long, I had a highly-developed sense of self-preservation when it came to opportunities for looking even more ridiculous than I did already.

'I understand,' said the woman, 'and in the meantime here's a brochure that will tell you all about what we do. Call me when you've spoken with your parents.' She smiled reassuringly again and then disappeared into the Copenhagen crowds. I wasn't used to feeling so excited and for a moment I felt suspended in unreality before the world started to turn again and I became aware of the background noise in the square. Surely the rest of my class from school were hiding around here somewhere and they were about to jump out and tell me that it was all another joke at the expense of the giraffe? But they failed to materialise. The rest of the town went about its business and the universe appeared to be functioning as normal.

Susanne looked at me as if she too couldn't quite believe what had just happened. She was the pretty one, but she wasn't mean-spirited. 'Gitte, you've got to do it!' she said. 'That's amazing!' She was really happy for me and grabbed my hand warmly. I loved Susanne – she was the only girl I knew who I could really trust.

By now it was getting quite late and we had to run to catch the bus to make my father's deadline. I spent the entire journey looking at every poster we passed. Beautiful women everywhere, each one advertising a different product. They were in the bus, on the streets, high up on the buildings…smiling, flawless creatures from another planet. With a lurch of disappointment I realised that the chance meeting had to be a big mistake; they couldn't ask me to be a model. How could I be up there? At this I glanced through the brochure again and now I thought about it, the production was a little cheap. I was preparing myself for the worst and this was my way of making the evidence fit the low expectations I always had for myself.

My parents were incredibly positive about the news. Even my dad, who had always had a conventional life and as an engineer was practical and orderly, was pleased. He knew that I'd finished the 10th grade at school with top grades and he gave his permission for me to follow up the invitation after a long conversation with Trice Thomsen, the director of Copenhagen Models. They agreed that I would go into the agency the following week to have a few test photos done.

'If you feel like doing it,' said Dad, 'I think you should.' It was a done deal.

Jan thought the sound of a door opening into the modelling world was the most fantastic thing he had ever heard. I'm not entirely sure he was thinking only of me. Two years younger, he was then in the middle of puberty and I have a feeling he was interested in making the most of sharing the limelight with a big sister with lots of gorgeous modelling friends.

I sat on the bus to Copenhagen Models with just my mum and the butterflies in my stomach for company. They took a series of black-and-white Polaroids and I had to fill out endless forms. Then there was nothing to do but wait. Trice Thomsen wrote to say that she couldn't promise anything but she would do what she could. 'You have the perfect body,' she explained, 'but just because you look great in person it doesn't mean that you will work in photos. But I'm sure you have it in you.'

She was right. Things started to move at an incredible rate. There were more professional tests soon after the first visit to the agency and within two weeks of that first meeting on Gråbrødre Torv, I was offered a job. I found it hard to keep up with what was happening: I'd seen those Polaroids and I thought I looked utterly ridiculous. I've no idea what I was expecting. Perhaps I thought that I'd be transformed into the potential model that Marianne Diers had seen, but even though the tests looked more professional I was wearing the same old clothes I always had and I had the same old face. Who'd want that?

Everything for Women wanted it, as it turned out. This was a Danish lifestyle magazine with interviews and fashion features. With the help of a fantastic Swedish photographer called Steen Andersson, I was about to become one of their most important models. My mother came along to the first shoot and I desperately wanted to hold her hand, though I knew I couldn't do that now I was a proper model. But the other girls were so beautiful: they looked so relaxed and professional; they knew exactly what they were doing. I could tell they knew how stunning they were. But I had no idea what I was supposed to do and I felt so ugly next to them – I was still waiting for someone to take me to one side to tell me that it had all been a misunderstanding.

I had to do my own make-up like everyone else – only the very top models could command a stylist and make-up artist. But I'd never bothered with it before: I didn't have friends to practise with and I never thought that part of a woman's life would be for me. While other girls were trying on outfits with each other, I was out riding or daydreaming in the countryside, so I didn't have a clue.

The other models had huge bags filled with products. I'd only brought some eyeliner and lipstick. All I could do was watch carefully and copy as best I could. The results looked as if a toddler had been raiding her mother's toiletries. As my mum always did, I put lipstick on my cheeks but I looked as if I was auditioning to be a zombie extra in a horror movie. It was catastrophic. Even though everyone had a laugh, the other models were really helpful: they corrected my technique, gave me advice and showed me how to do things.

We did that first shoot by the lakes in Copenhagen and it was ice-cold. I was wearing a thin shirt by the designer Ivan Grundahl and I had wet hair. At first I felt like I was freezing to death, but I soon blanked that out because I was excited and everything was so confusingly new. I warmed up as we finished off the shoot in Steen's atelier and I began to feel a bit more confident. The light was right, the clothes felt good and the photographer was amazing – I even began to think that my face looked okay.

For the first time in my life I felt a spark inside me. *You look all right*. 'Could it be?' I asked myself. I looked at my pictures and then I looked again at the other models. And I thought – I belong. Finally I was no longer an outsider. I'd spent a day with girls as tall and thin as I was: we were a herd of giraffes together and there was nobody around to make fun of us. None of us needed to stoop in shame. We stood up straight and we looked directly into the camera. Could life really work like this? I couldn't remember a time when I hadn't been a figure of fun. Now I was being paid to be myself.

CHAPTER 5

AN EDUCATIONAL EXPERIMENT

Let's go back a bit and take a look at me in my eighth grade. It was 1977 and I was at last about to change school. I'd spend the last couple of years before exams at 16 following a state-run experimental way of teaching. There was only one of these in the whole of Denmark and it was near where I lived. I was one of only a few students in the country to be asked to attend.

Everything was done differently – the building was new, the teachers were not traditional and the students weren't conventional either. The 48 students selected from some 50 schools had all had problems in their own way with their schooling. This new place was supposed to make learning a more positive experience and, more widely, to change the face of Danish teaching itself. It was hard to be a sensitive child in most Danish schools – you were supposed to fit in and conform. This was the Danish way: don't think you're better than anyone else. It was supposed to be all about equality, though in reality I think many Danes are just jealous if you do well.

But the '70s was a decade that would be renowned for experimentation and it was the turn of education. I'd spent so much of my time trying to feel like I was the same as all the other kids but my view of the world has always been more aesthetic. I think it's a very cool word: it comes from the Greek *aesthesis*. It's all about awareness of movement, feeling and the soul. This was everything that regular school was not about. Most Danes just want to know how to add up and subtract – don't breathe, don't feel, don't do anything! Don't try to analyse, create or understand more than is strictly necessary for survival. Don't take risks. It was the opposite of everything I felt. Everything was predictable and boring but this new school was much more in tune with the way I thought about things.

The new set-up allowed pupils to find their own way and they believed that it was important to develop your own personality. I found it fresh and different, as well as a little bit scary: the hierarchy had gone and we were free to think whatever we wanted. The daily fear and terror I'd faced earlier was no longer such a defining part of my life. Along with my new school came four things I'd never had before – music, tits, a boyfriend and a girlfriend. I started to live at last.

My dad had always told me to keep my music down, particularly on Sunday mornings. I was always singing – everyone was driven crazy by it, but I could never stop. I sang in my room, in the toilet, while I was cycling and particularly in the kitchen – the acoustics were great there.

Can you imagine how fucking annoying I must have been as a child, always singing? Because it was the '70s I'd be doing The Osmonds, a Danish artist called Sanne Salomonsen and more progressive Danish acts like Alrune Rod or Charlatan. My dad's taste was classical but hidden in his stack of vinyl were the guilty pleasures which I fell upon in the shape of big ballads by Elvis, Sinatra and Sammy Davis Jr. Songs like 'My Way' and 'You Ain't Nothing But a Hound Dog' still resonate deep inside me somewhere. As a teen, I'd have them on at ear-splitting volume. Belting out those songs was another way to forget the stresses of school life.

Books were also very important to me and through my mum at the library I was introduced to great authors from a very early age. By nine I was already reading works meant for adults and everything I couldn't experience because of all my physical problems, I consumed through books. They provided another welcome distraction from all that was wrong around me and the fear in the pit of my stomach.

My new school encouraged those things which I'd kept for myself as my own private escape route. They not only tolerated my energetic musical recitals but they *asked* me to sing. And I wasn't alone: many of the other pupils loved music and enjoyed performing. One of them was a boy named Christian.

At the centre of musical activity at school was Thomas Blachman. He was arrogant, eccentric and he thought he had a God-given talent for music – which he did. Many of the school's pupils went on to make names for themselves and Thomas is now the main judge on the Danish version of *The X Factor*. Back then Thomas and Christian were the archetypal '70s kids, smoking pot and being hippies while I was a preppie Olivia Newton-John and John Travolta-style kid with my ironed shirts. But I was attracted to their alternative lifestyle and it really freaked my parents out. I loved their music, though I remember that Thomas thought I was a complete idiot. He didn't think I could sing – he was completely into jazz, jazz, jazz, while I was little more conservative. Even so we had a great time and I began to fall for Christian.

He had dark hair, an open face and very defined cheekbones. His eyes were a beautiful green with strong eyebrows and his lips were full. Christian had the longest, prettiest hair I've ever seen on a boy: he was beautiful. Everyone thought he was the most fanciable boy in the school. I had fallen in love with him on the day I arrived, but I wasn't getting any interest myself. While my feelings were as strong as those of any developing girl, I was a late developer with the body of a kid: I was still the giraffe without the slightest sign of any boobs. I hadn't started my periods and I was basically just straight up and down. I'd never kissed a guy and I was longing to be experienced – I'd never got further than me and my showerhead.

When at last the physical changes of puberty came it was quick. Over just three months of the summer everything happened. Suddenly I looked like a woman and Christian was interested.

By then I had taken up smoking, having figured that if I didn't have boobs the next best things were cigarettes. Even the girls who were developed smoked. Anyone who was popular did. Your first time is always horrible but I was actually physically ill when I lit up and that developed into a nasty case of bronchitis. It didn't put me off and cigarettes helped my social life. I went on to hang out with the dope smokers, who would roll their joints in a secret hideout at school.

It was the first time I was unconditionally accepted as part of a circle, not counting the four-legged and assorted furry and feathered friends called Magic, Bella or Prins who had always seemed pleased to see me before. Over the two years at that experimental school I began to feel that I might just be good enough. It was a place filled with positivity, happiness, an inquiring spirit and learning was fun. Do you know, I still remember deciding to study the highland Indians of Peru and finding it to be totally absorbing in a way that work had never been before.

In the ninth grade I formed a band with Thomas and Christian and we performed Tina Turner's version of 'Proud Mary'. Later, I got to know Tina and we often laughed about my first effort and how it must have sounded coming from a tall, white teenager. She couldn't believe I'd pulled that one off and I didn't quite know what I was thinking either – I just loved her music. And it really worked. I felt like a rock star on that stage at school. I was in love with the bass player – Christian –while Thomas hated me (but what could he do?). My parents were there to see me perform, and I was so proud. They never came to the twice-yearly evenings to see how I was doing academically but that night they were finally in the audience.

Seeing me perform made my mother realise that I was going to do something different in my life. She had always known that I was bright and interested in reading and she'd got me my position at the local library. For a while I was working at both the library and the bakery on the same day and I enjoyed the roles. My mother imagined that I would go on to university and be a regular person. We had talked about me taking over the library from her and she had no reason to imagine that it wasn't what I wanted to go on to do: I loved books and I still do.

After my performance I made straight for my parents but my mum was quiet and her eyes were bright with tears. 'Gitte – you're going to be up on the stage for the rest of your life! I'm sure of it,' she said. 'You'll never be a librarian.' I couldn't have wished for a better appreciation, but she was shocked by how into it I was because I'd always been immersed in literature; I'd even made cassettes for people who couldn't read themselves. As a young kid it had been me who would read to the other children of my age – I was a natural.

But now I was lost to the adrenalin kick that came with performing live. I pictured myself on stage singing my own songs to thousands of fans all screaming my name. I'd travel by limousine and be a huge star. I was to get some of that fame, but just not with my music in the way I imagined back then.

I've tried a couple of times to make it in that world, but I didn't have the energy or the drive necessary to make it work. As a kid, music was everything. You wouldn't know my favourite song at the time outside Denmark. It was '*Lidt Til Og Meget Mer*' from the film *Mig og Charly* and the lyrics just seemed to be about my life. And in a very real way, they were. Even now I can't read them without getting goose bumps. The song was written by Kasper Winding, a musician who came from an incredibly talented family who were very famous in Denmark. Kasper worked with everyone from Bryan Ferry to Frank Zappa, but what I couldn't know as that eager young singer taking her first steps was that within five years, he would be my husband.

CHAPTER 6

OUT IN THE WORLD

I lasted two days at university. The grades that got me there had been excellent but I might as well still have been at school. Education was what my parents wanted for me but I was being stared at openly again and I knew it wasn't going to work out. I couldn't take all the bullshit and start from scratch as the awkward giraffe trying to do her best to be accepted; I wasn't even sure what I wanted to study.

I was still only 16, very young to be at university, and modelling looked as if it could be my way out. If I left Denmark for a couple of years, I thought, worked abroad and picked up some other languages, I would actually get points to add to my degree when I returned. My decision didn't exactly delight my parents, but we agreed that it could be beneficial to do a couple of years out in the real world to find out what I really wanted to study. I had their blessing.

My father's practical attitude was something I would be

forever grateful for. His regular existence gave him no idea as to what I might be heading into and yet he didn't try to stop me. Even though I was only a teenager he was prepared to let me be grown-up enough to leave home and explore the world. It was everything I'd dreamed of. Finally, I was going to be one of those birds I'd watched for so many hours.

I didn't think about the loneliness of the life I was choosing: I didn't imagine what it might mean when my mother and father weren't there or when handsome Italian playboys tried to pass me cocaine and told me, 'It's great, nothing to worry about – you'll feel wonderful!' My family wouldn't be able to give me a big hug when I'd gone to my hundredth audition and got yet another curt rejection. There would be no home-cooked backup to save me from going hungry because once more I hadn't made enough money to eat.

My head was filled only with the months I'd spent doing Danish catalogues and fashion shoots with friendly photographers who all told me how great I was, how beautiful I looked and how fabulous I seemed. I'd taught myself how to work the light and how to pose and look effortless: you have to be able to work at positioning yourself and be in harmony with the camera. Though I couldn't explain it, I found that I naturally picked up techniques that could take others years to perfect – I just seemed to be born with whatever skill was required and I hardly needed to learn anything at all. You see the same thing with footballers who have a certain innate rhythm and approach to their game which works. They instinctively know how to position themselves on the field in just the right place – and either you can do that or you can't.

I still remember the first cheque I received the week after I made my debut as a model. The library and the bakery had paid a little bit of money – and I mean tiny – and half of that I gave to my dad. But there was something different about my first proper pay and I really felt I was very cool: I had made money out of something that I had always thought I didn't have in me. It was just a couple of hundred *kroner* (Danish crowns), which back then was probably worth something in the region of £100–120. I'd earned in a day what would have taken me months in the bakery. But the amount wasn't important: it was the envelope with the modelling agency's stamp – the official stamp! I ran through the house to find my mum and show her the cheque.

'Okay,' she smiled, 'but you'd better put that in the bank – or at least save half and you can use the rest for something important.' Something important! Of course, I immediately called Susanne and we took the bus to Gråbrødre Torv, where we each had a whole beer to ourselves. This time we weren't going to have to share. I saw a short-sleeved shirt that I'd wanted and I bought that too. My family had never been well-off and sometimes my grandmother made jumpers for me – with an uncanny instinct for using the most revolting colours possible – and this was the first time I hadn't had to settle for buying clothes in the sales. Back in the '70s there'd been a brief period when these square-flared trousers had been popular. I finally got a pair two years after they peaked and I looked like a joke. Now I not only had some money but the fashion industry was becoming my world and I knew exactly what to buy.

I savoured the whole experience. No longer a window-shopper, I walked into one of Copenhagen's top stores, ignored the sale rack and took my time over the latest range of blouses. Quite a few of those first cheques went on clothes and shoes. I bought more than I needed: buying was proof that I was successful. None of those bitches who had made my life a misery at school would have ever thought I would get so far. It was like saying, 'See! You made fun of me, but look who's wearing the clothes now! Look who's walking the walk.' I felt slightly drunk with it all. They'd teased me mercilessly and now I was making more money than their parents. Revenge was a dish best served with a designer label.

I was walking at my full height when I went out with my mother in the centre of Rødovre, where I'd been used to being laughed at. I was, to be honest, probably a total pain in the ass – I must have been impossible. I'd got it and now I was flaunting it everywhere. But looking back, I forgive myself because it was a feeling that had been a long time coming and was well-deserved, though I do feel sorry for everyone who had to put up with me.

My new world was in complete contrast to everything that had gone before. It was almost comical. Now I couldn't be tall enough – the magazines even had me in high heels to make me look that bit higher. My skinny body wasn't a source of amusement, but something to be admired and desired. Had I not been so thin, the agency told me, they would never have signed me up. I'd never seen it as an asset at all and I had never done anything to make sure I was thin – I'd actually been trying to put on some weight because I felt so embarrassed about being under-developed. In my last school I wore three pairs of trousers in an attempt to make myself look like the other girls of my age. Pulling them all on was always time-consuming and uncomfortable but I was desperate to make up for the lack of shape I was now being told was my best feature.

Other girls suffered with horrendous diets to keep their weight down and I came across eating disorders everywhere I went. What I naturally had and hated for so long they were desperate to emulate. I did have some symptoms of anorexia at times in my career as a result of being naturally thin but some of my girlfriends in the modelling world have never overcome their disorders and a few have died as a result of anorexia.

All of us were on the borderline of what the World Health Organisation (WHO) defined as malnourishment. They applied this definition to anyone with a BMI (Body Mass Index) of under 18.5 in the developed world or under 15 in Africa. A model of 175cm weighing 56 kilos would have a BMI of 18.2. In the fashion world that was normal and considered quite sane. Most of the models in my time were closer to having a BMI of 15 – and that's when you start risking your life. But I never thought about it at the time and I maintained my weight without the endless miserable diets and strange lives of regular girls in modelling. I felt good, I looked good and the agency told me they had big plans.

Marianne Diers had signed me in Gråbrødre Torv to Copenhagen Models, but they had global connections. They worked very closely with Elite Models in New York owned by John Casablanca. 'We have a fantastic new girl in Denmark,' Marianne told him. 'Her name is Gitte and she is ready to go all the way to the top.' She sent pictures of me to New York and John gave me the thumbs-up.

Their idea was to give me a flavour of how modelling worked internationally by getting me to make a name for myself in Hamburg for a couple of months. A new set of photographers and their clients would prepare me for fashion week in Paris which would, so everyone hoped, be my big debut on the world stage of modelling. The agency were confident that I would be a star and the way they explained it, nothing could go wrong.

My mum kissed me goodbye and I boarded the night train to Germany on a bitterly cold winter evening in 1980. The agency had paid my fare and apart from the address of a shared apartment in Hamburg, I had very little in my purse. But that didn't matter – I was going to be a fantastic success and I firmly believed it would happen just as it had been described. My dreams were fuelled by the romantic evening I'd spent the night before when Christian and I said goodbye. In my mind I was certain that the two of us would spend the rest of our lives together. I felt an all-consuming love and I could see it was the same for him. I wasn't going to be away that long and it wouldn't mean anything. We were sure that what we had could certainly survive all that.

Put to the test, it wouldn't be long before I discovered that I wasn't actually that good at making long-distance relationships work. My love needed so much fuel that it would quickly flicker out without constant attention, but on the train that night all I knew was the world was waiting for me and so was the perfect boy.

The train pulled into Hamburg in the early hours and

things immediately began to look different. It was snowing and I had to make my own way to the apartment. Nobody answered the door, so the first few hours of my promising new life were spent slumped on the stairs outside with my suitcase. My confidence and excitement were frozen out of me and I felt lost, stupid and too young to be away from everyone I knew. I cried through sheer cold and exhaustion. It wasn't until after 8 o'clock that someone finally woke up and let me in.

There were another five girls who lived in the agency-owned apartment and all of us aspiring models had to bust our asses from first thing to get assignments. My Danish success meant little here. We would be called up for endless 'go-sees', the model equivalent of an audition. When my limited portfolio of Denmark pictures was picked for a job I would be called in so they could check me out. They barely looked up before saying, 'No.' Again and again it happened: Hamburg was my first taste of rejection. I'd never struggled as a model before. It was cold, that curt, bored, 'No – next', 'No good – next!', 'Wrong smile… too thin… too fat…' You could be in and out in less than 60 seconds. Dogs at Crufts are treated with more dignity. The humiliation was rolled into days trying to find my way around the city by bus, sweating to make sure I wasn't a second late for an agency who would immediately throw me out and on to the next disappointment.

When I began to get work it was mostly in catalogues. Hardly glamorous, 14-hour assignments, but the money was very good and it began to restore my self-esteem. I'd been thinking that I was back at school again, the giraffe starting to raise her long neck uncertainly inside me and I had been losing the battle with every successive 'No' to push her back down into her place.

The reality of modelling is that it's tough and degrading. There is nothing emotional in it, no heart. I couldn't feel sorry for myself for being looked at as if I was no more than the clothes I was wearing. The choice was between giving up or developing an attitude which told the world I didn't need anyone but myself. That's what I did in the end: stand up straight, walk tall, smile, thank them as they're saying get lost, dash to the next gig. Inside I crumbled and when I did manage to get a job there was the constant terror that it might be the last.

Agency waiting rooms were packed with groups of girls sobbing together uncontrollably. Aspiring models of 14 to 15 shook nervously as they listened out for the call that would lead to the big breakthrough or the next slap in the ego. My years of being laughed at and bullied at school turned out to have been, in some ways, useful. It was so much more difficult for the girls who had always been thought of as the most beautiful to find out that they were just one face of many.

The agency was as happy as I was that my diary was being filled, but for them it was pragmatic: I represented an investment in terms of the expenses they covered for me in Germany. They were paying for my accommodation and were keen to see some dividends. If their patience ran out before my luck changed, I would be packed off back home to Denmark. That was another reason to feel great relief as things began to pick up, though I have to say that I did like the hectic lifestyle and even got a sort of thrill from the uncertainty that came with the life. I didn't mind working hard and even getting as far as Hamburg was further than I had managed before. Twice as big as Copenhagen, the town was very beautiful and as I got to know it, I felt myself to be very far away from where I'd grown up. I wasn't much of a clubber at that point, but for me it was enough to experience living in a different country. It didn't make things any easier, but I knew it was worth what I was having to do to be there.

Denmark wasn't that far away anyway, at least physically. It was only 160 kilometres to the border and at first I regularly took the train to see my family, though these visits did fall away as I adjusted to my adult existence. I had an instinctive feeling that I wasn't going to go home: I had found something that was more what I had become, something bigger. There would be more than just Hamburg, I felt sure, somewhere where there was more to learn about different ways of living life. There was more space in my life now, space in which the precious, intimate love I had felt for Christian was hopelessly diluted. That meant there was even less reason for me to want to head back north again. Now I was ready for the world – Paris.

I knew what it was like to work with major photographers: I was used to speaking in English and I knew John Casablanca still had plans for me. The agency told me I had that 10 per cent extra – whatever it was that marked out the superstar from every other hard-working model.

New York and Paris were the centres of the fashion

business and I knew that if I could break there, I could make a name for myself anywhere, but I had never been to France. Paris represented the ultimate in romance, beauty, sophistication and culture. French was the language of seduction and sounded like it too. The worst insult sounds sexy delivered in French and I had always wanted to master it.

Today I speak fluent Italian, English and German but I never did well in French, even at school. Me and France, it would turn out, were just never meant to be and maybe that's why I always struggled with the language. Despite my best hopes and the best plans of the agency, Paris was going to be a complete disaster: I never liked the French and the feeling was mutual. If I thought that Hamburg was hard, I was about to find out that the Paris I'd always hoped to see was only in my dreams.

CHAPTER 7

ALONE IN THE CITY OF LOVE

My new life in the capital of France filled me with huge expectation. Ever since I was a little girl the very name 'Paris' had come loaded with magic. I was jittery with anticipation when I arrived. The Danish agency were certain that Paris would fall before me and I felt sure that something wonderful was about to happen.

I wanted to see all the famous sights and looked forward to the buzz of seeing the town as a local. I'd be working and living there when I went up the Eiffel Tower rather than just being a tourist. I was filled with the romance of it all and couldn't wait to join the thousands who have scribbled their messages on Montmartre's love wall in languages from all over the world. In my mind I was already tripping through the sunny streets and watching life go by through an art-deco window in a bohemian cafe like I'd seen them do in a thousand films – the food, the shopping, visiting Versailles outside the city.

The spring was warm and it was great to be out on the streets when I got to see my first Sony Walkman. At 17, I felt young, beautiful and ready to conquer the city and I was incredibly impressed by the American model rollerblading through Parc Monceau with a big pair of headphones connected to this clunky, battery-powered tape player. I did a double-take and grinned, not quite believing he could listen to music while he was out. He looked so cool and this was exactly the sort of sophisticated display I had been expecting to see in fashion-conscious Paris. When I later found out the enormous price of those Walkman players I almost passed out. The future had arrived, I decided, though even that wasn't as expensive as the car phone I got to try around the same time. To this day my mother has never quite accepted that the excited call she got from me in Paris was really made on the move: the phones weren't even on the market.

I lived in an apartment with two other models in Montmartre. We were at the foot of the hill that leads up to the Moulin Rouge. Elite's headquarters were in the heart of the city in an old building. Inside you could expect to find top models such as Janice Dickinson, Jerry Hall and Gia – Gia Marie Carangi. Later portrayed in a movie about her life by Angelina Jolie, Gia's tragic life ended at the age of just 26. I remember her as a friend and someone who made a unique impression with her completely exclusive way of living. Constantly on the covers of *Vogue*, *Cosmopolitan* and many other fashion magazines, she was like a goddess in her photoshoots, but I was shocked when I saw her early one morning before the make-up artist had got to her. There was a young, lost soul screaming in pain which could only be anaesthetised through a shot of heroin. Her eyes were sunken and black and she was shaking. I'd seen nothing in my limited experience like it, no film depiction of addiction had ever looked as bad as that; it was very scary.

Gia had the world's photographers around her from the day she started in New York. The little bisexual boy/girl from Philadelphia never had the tough skin that modelling needed and she paid for it with her life. On 18 November 1986, she died of AIDS – and hardly anyone noticed. Her story made her famous but by the time she was acknowledged for being the world's first supermodel it was too late. I would think of her again when I started to poison myself with my own addiction.

While I was in Paris I would get yearning letters from Gia. She poured out her love for me, which just made me really embarrassed. There was no problem for me with being gay and it was quite accepted in Denmark but it just felt strange that she was attracted to me. My letters in return were guarded, as friendly as I could make them knowing that I couldn't give her the response her vulnerability needed. I had a sense of self-preservation that helped me to toughen up enough to survive the world in which we were both trying to find our way.

Paris and I had a far less harmonious relationship. We were speedily heading from honeymoon to irreconcilable differences after just a few months. My working life had become a living hell, far worse than anything I'd encountered in Germany. I felt every inch the giraffe again and I began to suffer panic attacks. 'Who do you think you are?' the bookers said. Here it was again. 'You're too skinny…' 'What do you *look* like?' 'Your hair is terrible!' 'How *dare* you come here with three pictures in your portfolio!' 'Just get out!' I was pushed around verbally and physically. It wasn't like they were just dismissive, they seemed actively angry at the way I looked when I turned up. I kept asking myself what was wrong with me: I secured not a single job, not one.

Catalogues had been reliable standby jobs before but now even their bookers were looking at me as if I had marched in through the wrong door. Within weeks I was back to crying myself to sleep. I still dreamed that my handsome prince would ride up and save me – but these days he no longer spoke French. The exhaustion and depression manifested themselves as physical symptoms. My hair started to fall out, my lips were raw with cold-sores. In turn, this look did little to improve my chances at the few casting sessions I was still getting.

Paris made me feel as if I were a waste of everyone's time. I was as total a flop as I had been promised I would be a superstar. Each day that passed ran up more bills for the modelling agency. What a fiasco, what a failure!

'But you've just started here in Paris, Gitte. There's no model who would get work the day they arrive. Keep your head – it'll be okay.' This was Monique, the director of Elite in Paris. She tried to get my spirits up. Monique had played the mother hen role for some of the most beautiful models in the world, but they were out there making piles of money and after two months of absolutely nothing I was all ready to pack up and go home. I was spent. My interest in the work had gone with my energy. I was feeling homesick. It just wasn't meant to be for me in the fashion world: I was what I had grown up as – a skinny creature who didn't fit in. The agency was supportive – they also didn't want to see their investment disappear to Denmark.

Monique called John Casablanca in New York. 'You just wait and see – she's going to be a superstar. I've seen her pictures,' he said. 'Perhaps we just need to set her up somewhere else.' He was just about to fly over to Paris anyway and he promised that he would come up with a new plan.

The very next day I was called in to a meeting with John himself. He thought I would have better luck in Italy, where the designers were more progressive. 'Why don't you pack your bags?' he said. 'We can fly out this evening.' He continued with a few casually-delivered hints as to how I might improve my chances, which coming from him sounded very much like orders.

'Do something about your look. You have a fabulous face, but we need to do something different... Cut your hair short, buy some new clothes, change your shoes...' He handed me $2,000. And that was that. In that moment, everything changed – about me and about my career. I got my hair cut boyishly short and had it bleached, and that became my iconic look.

We flew from Paris that day and John presented me to his Milan agency with the implied expectation that I would be respected by them and they would work hard for me. He called all his contacts in Italy and told them the new girl in town was one to watch. That night we spent together in the hotel. I remember thinking John was so old – I mean, for me at 17, he just seemed impossibly ancient. I wasn't even fluent in English, and I had a boyfriend back in Denmark. But it was also the point at which my career began to take off.

Suddenly everyone was crazy about my Scandinavian look and my short hair; I was the new trend everywhere. Milanese designer Luciano Soprani was huge in the '80s. He's since passed away but back then he worked with Max Mara, Heliette, Basile, Nazareno and Gabrielli, all key figures in Italian fashion. Luciano hired me when he was head designer for Gucci and he was crazy about me. And because *he* was crazy about me, everybody else wanted me. The assistants at the modelling agency hardly had time to keep up – Giorgio Armani, Gianni Versace... everyone was calling for me. I travelled to exotic locations for photoshoots in private jets and might be having brunch with Mick Jagger one morning and tea with Prince Albert of Monaco the same day. This was the genuine big-time. And I was still only 17.

When you go fast in modelling, you go *really* fast. Everything was bigger, better... it was an effort to remember it all but I tried because here was my dream becoming reality and it was all happening at once. Mostly it was all good, it was really fun. I met some incredible people and I quickly got used to the VIP lifestyle. However, when things went wrong, I thought I was going to die.

That was 1981. Ever since then I have had problems with loud sounds. Even the noise of something so innocuous as the boiler going on can be terrifying and I can't stand fireworks on New Year's Eve. The cause was what had seemed to be nothing more threatening than a prestigious campaign to promote Fila bikinis in the beautiful Seychelles islands in the Indian Ocean, off the east coast of Africa. I was really excited to have been chosen.

Along with four other models I flew from Milan direct to the island of Mahe. We were driven to an amazing resort on the far side. A delegation from Fila greeted us and the five of us bikini models were treated like rock stars. We had two days to relax, have cocktails and we were under instruction to be sure to sunbathe so that we had some colour on us. It was promising to be a very good gig.

One of the other models warned me and Nickie, an American girl who was, like me, very fair-skinned, to make sure that we didn't get too much sun on us. Of course, what did I do? Cocktails... sunshine... gossiping about boys... having fun. I was a wide-eyed Danish girl with a great body in a five-star resort and I was soaking it all up. After the two days I was covered in sunburn. The photographer freaked out.

'We're supposed to be shooting, just go and get that seen to! Get some cream or something,' he said. 'We start tomorrow morning.' I was too young to have got a Danish driving licence and Nickie said she'd drive me. The photographer told us to use the hotel jeep as the Seychelles didn't have much infrastructure at that time. There were just three main resorts on the whole island and the nearest decent shops were on the other coast.

For me at that age even being driven in a jeep was an exciting adventure in itself. We weren't likely to get lost as there was only one proper tarmac road and that took us past the airport again. As we got near it, we passed a truck full of locals. They were all screaming in French – the Seychelles having once been controlled by France. I'd picked up very little French during my unhappy sojourn in Paris and had absolutely no idea what they were telling us, but it was clear they were not happy. To me as an ignorant young thing in paradise their attitude struck me as unnecessary. 'Imagine being so angry in such a beautiful place,' I told Nickie. She was distracted by the petrol station inside the airport perimeter and decided to take what might be her only opportunity to fill up before we went on with our shopping.

As Nickie paid for the fuel two men approached us. They were both white, which was unusual enough on the island. More ominously, they were sweaty, clearly irritated and each carried a machine gun. A big machine gun each. Nickie and I looked at each other before trying a smile and a 'Hi, how are you?' while failing to disguise our terror. These guys weren't even wearing uniforms and were clearly not police, much less regular army. We managed to get something out of them in English. There had been a coup. I later found out that the President of the Seychelles, France-Albert René, had instigated a Socialist government in a move that triggered the takeover.

'You've got very little time,' they said. 'See that doorway?' They pointed over to the tiny airport. We saw a small group of people about a hundred metres away, all running towards the entrance the men were pointing out. 'Go,' they said.

I don't know if we left our bags, I can't really remember much about the order of events. We started running towards the fence that separated the station from the check-in entrance. You normally had to make your way around it to get into the departure area but gunfire from somewhere behind us raked the ground and if we still had anything, we dropped it and screaming, fought our way over the fence and towards the door. The facilities at the airport were as basic as the resorts and the door we found looked like it might have belonged to a shabby office. As we pulled it shut behind us, the sound of bullets ceased.

We were definitely in some kind of administration area. It was quite a small room, certainly not big enough to comfortably contain the 40 or so people we were sharing it with and who right then were looking at us in terror. The furniture was old-fashioned and cheap. We were the only two white people in the room and given that the coup was being staged by whites, it seemed the others thought we were part of the attacking force. Although we tried to explain that we had nothing to do with what was going on, that we were just as much in trouble as they were, they didn't look as if they believed us.

There was an old English guy there who had taken shelter with his daughter. When we got talking to him he said that the attempt to take over the island could get very serious; the gunmen hadn't followed us but it felt like we had been thrown in a prison cell as surely as if the door had been locked. The heat would have been unbearable even if so many weren't jammed in together. It was 37 degrees and 80 per cent humidity with the only light coming from narrow windows running around the top of the walls of the room. There was no ventilation, no air conditioning and even though we couldn't see out of the room because the windows were set so high up, we could hear constant noise. Gunfire, explosions. The room glowed dull red with each blast and our nerves were increasingly shredded as time inched by.

At last the door was kicked open without warning by two men, one a redhead – originally from Holland, as I found out later. They were part of the mercenary force and both had machine guns. The redhead seemed particularly jumpy, sort of pumped up and angry. It seemed as if he was on something, like he was only just hanging on to his self-control. He was clearly ready to kill anyone who so much as looked at him the wrong way. For no reason I could make out – he hardly needed to scare us more – he shot out all the glass in the little windows above us. The noise of the machine gun in such a confined space was deafening. The room shook with the sustained burst of fire and you could feel the vibrations from the weapon judder through you. Some of the other hostages put their hands over their ears, everyone ducked, some screamed. It was chaos. Shattered glass rained down on us and when at last it was over, not a single window was left. The two men disappeared, leaving the group dazed, sobbing, crouched by the walls and sitting in broken glass.

We were abandoned without anything to eat and, more tellingly in the stifling heat, without any water. Hours passed and we lapsed into a kind of trance. One of the other women just cried continuously, another kept getting cramps, another was rocking and humming to herself.

Some time later the same two men came back, kicking the door open before they entered as if they really thought we might be ready to somehow overpower them. 'Don't try anything stupid!' the manic redhead shouted in English. I don't know how or if the locals could understand exactly what he was saying, but nobody had any plans to be heroes. 'We've taken over the whole island. If you try to leave this room you will be shot!' It was English and I didn't need to be fluent to understand what he meant.

I wasn't able to say exactly how long we had been held, but 10 hours or more must have passed. It was beginning to get dark outside and even from where we were lying on the floor we could see fire lighting up the evening somewhere outside the airport. There was no relief from the heat. It felt like the night was going to be even more humid than the day. The broken windows allowed in thick, humid air heavy with the smell of gun smoke and burning. Tension was beginning to give way to hysteria. A few of the group had diarrhoea. Whether they were ill already or it was just the shock was impossible to say. There was no toilet and the stench mingled with the sweat in the oppressive atmosphere and the sounds of weeping. From outside, gun battles continued as the light faded.

Would Mum and Dad have heard about the coup? How could I reach them? Nickie and I had curled ourselves up under an office table while almost everyone else was slumped against the far walls. The Englishman stayed near us but the rest kept their distance. In addition to the language barrier there was an increasing sense of a racial barrier between us. No matter how tired and scared and sweaty we looked, we were still the white girls and the stares were suspicious. The red-headed guy had looked at the others with particular viciousness; you could tell he really hated black people and I think they had us down as more like him. They seemed to be waiting for us to do something. And for my part, as it got darker I could make out little more than the eyes of the other hostages. Their skin colour became harder to make out for my overloaded senses. The noise was constant and the accumulated temperature over the day made the air thick and heavy.

There was a second door in the room which our English friend became convinced led to the toilet. 'Please don't try it,' I whispered, when he decided to crawl slowly over to open it. 'When they come in and shoot you, they'll shoot us too because we're here.' He did it anyway. I knew it wouldn't be a toilet and it wasn't. It opened onto a much smaller room, almost a cupboard. There was a kind of fax machine in there with its own keyboard. Rather than send a sheet of paper, you typed directly on the machine itself – and each key press was accompanied by a loud beep. We cringed at each sound as the English guy, watched by his anxious daughter and us beyond tried to get a message to the outside world.

In terror, we waited for the outside door to our prison to fly open and the sound of machine guns. That fucking machine! It chirruped away for what seemed like years. Our friend had a business card from his hotel on the island and he was faxing to say we were captives. We had no way of knowing whether or not the hotel was in the hands of the mercenaries; we might have just told our captors to come and kill us. At last he finished, the message was sent and at least something had been done. We were all so tired, apart from anything else. The constant fear, the uncertainty was sapping what little energy we had left. We could talk only in low voices. A new and louder series of beeps from the fax in the other room announced a reply.

We looked at one another helplessly. There was no way of stopping the machine if anyone outside heard, but fortunately the message was very short. It revealed that the island wasn't totally under the control of the mercenaries; there were a dozen in all from Holland and we found out later that they'd pretended to be baseball players. The cases for their bats contained guns and when they were discovered at the airport they shot their way out. Their plan was being put into action that morning just as we turned up to buy petrol and saw them in their casual baseball outfits. A rescue force from South Africa had already flown in to retake the territory. They were engaging the mercenaries in battle and said they would rescue us within 12 hours. It was fantastic news but it seemed a long way off. I felt so sick I wasn't sure I was going to make it much longer.

When the door was next kicked open the men didn't come in themselves, but they did throw in a six-pack of Coke. It was a callous joke – six cans between 40. They would have been better to give us nothing. I'd like to say that it was rationed depending on need, but the truth was that 40 desperate hostages climbed over each other to get to the warm drinks. I had no chance. I became convinced that I was going to die in here. *How can we survive? We're not even helping each other*, I thought. You hope that when you find yourself in an emergency that you behave with dignity and bravery, but you never know what you're going to do beforehand. When someone's got a gun to your head, you react instinctively. There's something deep inside you which tells you what to do and you can plan.

But this was another time when I could swear that I had a guardian spirit watching over me. A fierce orange glow lightened the room and more smoke drifted through the windows. A young girl next to me seemed to make up her mind. 'Fire,' she said. 'We're going.' She pulled open the door. There was no discussion, no more waiting in fear as cans of drink were discarded on the floor. *Let's run*, we all thought. Everyone got to their feet and without looking to see who might be waiting, we pushed through the main door.

Less than two hours had passed since we read the fax confirming help was on its way. It was too dark and confusing to see exactly what was going on but I could tell from the explosions where the battle for the airport was being fought. We were caught in the middle and our group scattered in panic as each of us chose whichever direction seemed most likely to lead to safety.

I focused on three figures I could just about make out who looked as if they were in uniform, pulling Nickie along with me. Another one of our group kept up until he dropped to the ground right next to us: he'd been shot. And the thing that haunts me to this day is that Nickie and I kept going – we didn't stop for him, we ran. I don't know what happened to him but I think he probably didn't make it.

The two of us soon reached the men who were indeed from the military. They had commandeered an ambulance and knocked out its windows. We lay on the floor and they took us at high speed to a hospital on the other side of the island.

The men were heavily armed. Nowhere was safe at this point and they didn't know where the invading force was.

The hospital had nothing to treat us for shock and we ended up with coffee – probably not what our nervous systems needed but we were grateful for any liquids by then. We sat quietly and watched as patients were wheeled in, among them a local boy who couldn't have been more than eight. He had a gaping hole in his stomach. It still wasn't safe for us to be so close to the fighting and as soon as we were up to it, we were moved to a hotel in a secure area.

The American counsel and assorted dignitaries were already there. They'd been transferred from their quarters in time. My first thought was for my parents. I begged the US authorities to let them know I was okay. We learned that the airport was badly damaged, phone lines were out and a 24-hour lockdown had been imposed. The 12 mercenaries had been killed, but none of us were allowed to move from the hotel.

I was still very scared and shocked and would jump when anyone so much as knocked over a glass. It seemed as if we were hiding in our accommodation forever, though it was probably less than a week before the curfew was relaxed. At last we could go back to our photoshoot and get on with the job.

But when we returned, the photographer was furious.

'Where have you fucking been?' he shouted. 'This campaign is costing us a fortune and you never got in touch once to say what was going on!' Miserably I thought to myself that this was almost worse than what I'd been through. If I'd been older I'd like to think I'd have slapped him back much harder. As it was I started to explain, stumbling over my words, but he didn't let me finish. They knew all about the coup, he said dismissively. His only concern was that I should have tried harder to get a message through to them. *The fucking phone lines were down!* I thought, but he just didn't get it. What could I do? I got back to work.

We worked from early morning until 11.30am when the light became too strong and we broke until 4pm: you'd get the best light and finish around 7pm. In the last couple of days of the shoot I became sick – probably as a result of the conditions I'd been held in at the airport. Despite that I still think some of the photos were pretty good. There was one of me draped over a palm tree, the curve of its trunk contrasting with the arch of my body; you wouldn't know what I'd been through. I look back at that and admire the resilience I had when I was young, or at least how well I was able to disguise the fact that I was about to drop with exhaustion... My fever hit 42 degrees before I was totally laid out.

I wasn't recovered by the time we were due to fly back, but the Seychelles government had just declared that you couldn't travel if you were ill. I had to pretend to be a hundred per cent healthy in the little orange shorts and T-shirt that were the only clothes I'd brought with me. I shivered my way through customs and did my best not to vomit, with the photoshoot crew all the while hissing at me to stand up straight and look relaxed.

I made it onto the plane which was to go to Frankfurt, where we would change for Milan. It was winter in

Germany. Snow fell and nobody offered to help me when we disembarked to board the transfer bus. I shivered uncontrollably waiting for everyone to get on for the short ride. The photographer looked at me contemptuously. 'You stupid little girl,' he said. 'You knew how cold it would be here. Why didn't you wear something else?' I cried, silently. I didn't say anything to him but I promised myself I'd never go back to the Seychelles – and I never have.

Mum and Dad were waiting for me in Milan. There they were, smiling faces at last! The American Counsel had managed to make contact and the media back home had reported, 'The Danish hostage has been reported to be okay,' which was when they knew. My then boyfriend, Luca, was also there to meet me. We celebrated, but I got back to work all too quickly. If something like that happened now I am sure I would be in post-traumatic stress counselling straight away. Who knows, I might not have gone on to develop my problem with noise. I did get over it for a while and it's only as I get older that I find it's come back. Perhaps I think about things more these days.

The modelling agency were happy to see me back, at least superficially. As far as they were concerned I had survived so now I could get on with my job. They never really asked me what had happened; that was the modelling world all over. You're back! You're still gorgeous! So now get with the programme... it's a new day today, baby!

CHAPTER 8

LIFE AT THE TOP

My success as a model never fulfilled me, though I grew up fast, got to see some amazing places and became friends with famous people. I'd done more than most girls had by their late teens and I had all the things I'd never been able to afford when I was growing up, but I was beginning to discover that it didn't compensate for feeling the emptiness of the business I was in. Instead, it actually made it seem worse.

I wasn't lonely, there were always people around me, but I was still as solitary as I had been as a child; I couldn't seem to learn how to reconcile those two parts of me. And that's because I loved the lifestyle in many ways – I do love having nice things around me, I liked all the trappings and the glamour of being known wherever I went. When I finished a shoot one day, went out to a club and sat next to Robert De Niro it wasn't an unusual evening. I loved to flirt and to dance and I hardly ever drank. Drugs were never my thing

– I tried cocaine on just two occasions but I never had the taste for it, which was a good thing because it was everywhere. It was like being a rock star at the nights I went to in the '80s. You could have anything you wanted; it was a time of excess and piles of coke were put out as if they were bowls of crisps at a cocktail party.

I was happy with the way I looked and when I wasn't working, I felt freedom under my wings: I was the bird who had finally flown away. My dancing was wild and I was Danish – you know, I didn't wear a bra – but I didn't want that to mean I was available. A lot of men misunderstood – they thought it was an invitation to something more. And it never was, it just wasn't, but I loved the attention; I liked having people notice me for all the right reasons. Off duty I was a tease and I just wanted to have fun. I'd got used to being praised for my great ass and my beautiful boobs – and I appreciated every moment of it.

I was good at the job, I was professional and agents knew that when I said, 'Yes,' to a job, I meant it. I worked even under the most difficult circumstances. It wasn't enough just to have a great body either: I took care of myself and I could transform in front of the camera. Health, strength and discipline were vital to keep up with the demands of modelling. I was up at 5.30am, in the studio by 7am and working through until 9pm. I couldn't have gone out partying all the time and going off to get fucked up without it having an effect on my ability to work; I ensured I was always on top of my game and constantly in demand.

Everything went in a blur but I do remember being asked to do a shoot for Rolex. I wasn't feeling very well that morning but the agent countered this by saying I'd be working with Helmut Newton. Suddenly, I felt better again! The chance to work with the legend and his wonderful wife June was too much and I didn't need to ask anything else. Most fashion photographers do their best with light and clothes to make you look beautiful but it's all very formulaic. Helmut demanded expression and feeling. He was direct, powerful and had an unassailable sincerity in his approach. You would end up in front of the camera with your limbs at angles which shouldn't possibly have worked, but somehow he brought life and playfulness to every shot.

It was the same with Herb Ritts. Both were creative and demanding in a way that felt refreshing. There was always a sense of a story behind their set-ups but neither of them ever spelled it out while they were shooting. Working with them was more exhausting than regular shoots but also tremendously inspiring. Their assignments were all the more welcome because they didn't come along that often and served to highlight the mediocre filler I had to do between times. I was easily bored and it hadn't taken long for me to realise that modelling at any level quickly became routine: I needed something more artistic to keep my attention.

My days were usually busy but virtually interchangeable. By the time I was on set first thing, I would have had a bath and done legs, eyebrows, nails… everything perfect. I'd say 'Hello' to the photographer, get with the make-up artist, stylist… On with the first set of clothes and repeat various parts of the same old performance all day – with a half-hour for lunch. I was a highly-paid clothes hanger, which is, of course, the job, but it wasn't very interesting. Some models go on as long as possible, but while I don't mean to suggest I was better than them, I guess the shine quickly faded.

The groupies could be particularly annoying. Girls had to watch out for handsome young playboys with good clothes, fast cars and practised charm. I instinctively knew that there was something to be wary of, but a lot of my girlfriends didn't – particularly the Americans. We'd go to exclusive clubs where you paid an unbelievable amount of money to secure a table. The American girls would be demure and prim sitting down and reserved in their dancing, yet they'd always leave with the boys. 'All that "shy" bullshit,' I said to another of my friends when yet another left arm-in-arm with a charmer, 'what's that all about?' I'd been an outsider for so long at school that I didn't need the company.

There was also something a bit tragic about the playboys. They were more to be laughed at than swept off my feet by but they weren't bad people on the whole, though. I thought they were flattering and nice, apart those who had been doing it so long that they were getting a bit old and creepy, but they were revered in Italy. There, it was a serious business – a career for some of them. They had impeccable manners and their sole goal was to service the young models; that was basically their thing. What wasn't so widely known was that they were paid by modelling agencies – even the wealthy lads. Their job was to keep the girls busy when they felt lonely. The models were either working hard or on the treadmill looking for assignments. They'd be distracted by the boys, they might have a little coke and most of the time, they didn't care when they didn't make it. How could you resist a gorgeous guy when you were 17 and blue?

How it worked was the agency let new models know where the best clubs were located and these were the ones they packed out with their young men, champagne and exclusive areas. Used up after two or three years, most of the girls were never heard of again. The girls who didn't come from Italy were the most vulnerable: they were in a strange land where they didn't speak the language, maybe a continent from home and they weren't really able to make a proper judgement about who they could trust. It was the side of the industry that didn't get written about in the fashion editorials.

My daily conversations with my dad helped me in resisting the politics of the business. He underlined how important it was to call regularly and I always told him how I was doing and what problems I faced. He was so practical and always had a solution. His attitude towards me was so much more relaxed than I ever thought it might be growing up in our strict household. The big clubs were open every night and some girls were out all the time but my money was more usually spent flying back to Denmark. It was only an hour-and-a-half from Milan with a short drive and those visits probably helped to keep me out of trouble.

The boyfriend I got not long after I established myself in Milan also helped me keep my feet on the ground. I met Luca in a club that had become a favourite because it wasn't plagued by playboys. The DJs were amazing and it wasn't really somewhere to drink, you just went in to dance. And that's how I met Luca.

There was something about him, though he wasn't as handsome as some of the guys who would always be hanging around: he had a big nose for a start and big lips. Luca was very fit but definitely not what you'd expect me to be into as a model. He was an amazing dancer though: watching him move really kicked something into life in me. Night after night we'd meet after 11pm and dance and dance until we couldn't any more and then we'd just go to sleep. I'd be up first thing in the morning for work. I was so happy; he was so natural and normal.

At first I didn't want anything more than to be his dancing partner. He would often ask me out for a pizza but for a long time I held back until he finally asked, 'Can I take you for a real dance?' That was it – finally he'd got me on a date and it seemed right that it was about dancing. I was excited because he wasn't like the regular Italian guys: he was straightforward and said we might go on afterwards to have something to eat with his parents. He was just a regular kid.

That evening we danced until 4 o'clock in the morning, then we slept together at his place – but it was only sleeping. We collapsed together on the bed and nothing more happened between us. I had to get up at 8am and Luca woke me, got my breakfast and drove me to the job. I was so used to everything in my world being a transaction that his kindness made me worry about what he expected in return. He picked me up and kept on doing that for the next couple of weeks. We'd have dinner together perhaps, but do nothing physical. It allowed time for me to get to know him and I didn't feel pressurised. I got to like him in a very easy way, but I didn't feel much more for him until one rainy day when I was late for work.

Luca took me on his bike, speeding through the busy streets of Milan. Visibility was bad and we almost came off. Steam poured off us as we arrived on that cold day and he took his helmet off. His long hair tumbled down and his glance back at me changed everything: the world went in slow motion. Something hit me inside and I fell in love; strange that all my doubts about his looks should disappear. I had fallen for an 18-year-old boy who lived with his parents in a very ordinary quarter of Milan. He spent his days playing tennis – he was very good and his family hoped he would be able to become a pro – and by night, well, we know. He danced.

I felt transformed. For weeks I'd thought nothing special about Luca except that we'd got on very well and we'd seen a lot of each other. We'd got hot and sweaty dancing, we'd had dinner with his parents but every echo in my soul had told me that he could never be someone I would go for. And now we were together, everything was bright and vivid and each day was beautiful.

I moved in with Luca and his family and for the next year my life was anchored. Luca drove me to work and every evening, whenever I wasn't away, we'd have delicious homemade pasta at their place before going out dancing. We went to football matches and visited the busy market that ran every third Saturday throughout the summer on the piazza nearby. Mercato dell'antiquariato di Brera was full of beautiful Italian antiques and Luca's neighbourhood was very bohemian. I thrive on the energy of cities, their sounds, their inhabitants and their smells.

Living with Luca provided a way of combining the high drama of modelling with the security of a warm home. His parents were very typical Italians, down-to-earth and loving. I didn't speak the language, so daily activity was accompanied by miming and picking up words as we went along. Luca was an only child and I became the daughter that his mother never had – she was very kind.

We spent a lot of time in San Siro, a very attractive part of the city packed with lovely cafes. There were shops selling expensive handmade clothes by top designers and the area was also known for its gigantic football stadium. I had limited time to enjoy it. Quite often I'd have to go back to Paris to do shoots or spend days on some exotic island and increasingly I was being asked to do a lot in the US. If it hadn't have been for Luca, I would probably have relocated to New York as the second fashion capital of the world after Paris, but it was still one of the happiest periods of my life, even though the constant travelling was a strain and in the end wore away at the relationship.

Towards the end of our year together, he and I began arguments which over time escalated into full-on fights. I was losing weight that I really couldn't afford to lose and was becoming irrationally jealous. I accused Luca of playing around. I became quite miserable and it couldn't last. I'll never forget the day we finally broke up. Meat Loaf was at the height of his pomp and Luca had a tape player in the tiny room that had been my home with him for getting on for two years. As I angrily pulled my clothes out from the small cupboard, I knew it was over. Luca put on 'Paradise By The Dashboard Light' from that timeless paean to doomed teenage love, *Bat Out of Hell*, which had provided a deafening soundtrack to millions of youthful bedroom dramas in the '80s.

I grabbed a handful of T-shirts and said goodbye to it all... the happy home... the dancing... the motorbike rides through Milan... everything we shared that meant so much. It hadn't been anything out of the ordinary, Meat Loaf articulated it so well, but it had been the world for me. I was at an age where everything seemed more emotional but in truth I do think it took me years to get over Luca.

My anxiety attacks returned. I didn't have anywhere I felt safe and although I threw myself into my work, I was very vulnerable. I got huge rushes of homesickness rising up through my body like a huge bubble. After one severe episode when I passed out, I ended up in hospital. My blood pressure went sky-high and I developed a fever. My mother flew in and the doctors told her I was suffering from stress. When I got out, I felt tired of everything: the superficial lifestyle of the model was hollowing me out. The constant travelling, the demands of casting agents and the agencies, the ever-present playboys, the photographers impatiently waiting for me the second I'd got off the latest plane. And I felt the lack of intellectual stimulation. Perhaps it was seeing my mum which reminded me of the love of books I'd grown up with; there had always been something new and interesting to absorb in the library. I was in need of that again. I wanted to be creative, to write songs, to see my family and to find stability again so I called the agency and told them it was over. Stop.

They had never heard anything so shocking: they told me

it was depression, that a lot of girls got the same way. I was at the height of my career, they said. I was 20 years old and I had an unrivalled portfolio. This, they informed me, would be a bad time to call a halt to my career. But I was serious. They kept on – I was earning so much money, I had so much work coming in.

'Are you bullshitting us?' they asked.

When I said, 'No,' I meant it. I got on a plane to Denmark: I wanted to find some peace and to work out what I was going to spend the rest of my life doing. It was time to think about picking up my studies again and maybe go back to university. The only thing that would stand in my way was my heart – as ever, it had its own plans for me and it was to insist on being heard.

CHAPTER 9

AND THE STONES PLAYED IN THE BACKGROUND

I arrived back in Denmark in 1983 and I was filled with plans for going back to university. I'd earned a lot of money in my years as a model. Once I'd got a few covers for magazines like *Vogue* under my belt, for which I'd earn as little as $50, I could get from $1,000 to $3,000 a day doing the really high-paying catalogue jobs. They only touch you after you've done the big fashion mags.

I hadn't kept a huge amount: a full 50 per cent of every job went straight to the agencies to start with. I'd also spent a lot on flights home and was always buying presents for friends and family. Then there were holidays in Ibiza with girlfriends, taxis and clothes. I didn't care because I had chosen to leave that life and what was important was being home again.

I had time before the academic year began and filled in the gap modelling in Denmark while I decided exactly what it was I was going to do in the long term. A campaign for Levis featured me in a stark photo wearing jeans and a plain, simple white T-shirt, one hand reaching for the sky as if I was carrying the world and one of my breasts was exposed. It became a huge success and there were massive posters everywhere. My mum just about passed out when she saw it.

I was treated like a conquering hero: I'd helped to make Denmark look cool to the rest of the world and when everyone sat up, I turned their requests down and came home. My career had the opportunities more usually only open to men; I could pick up work when I wanted and I was independent. When a smart new Copenhagen bar and restaurant called Cafe Victor – still going today – asked me to represent them, I did a publicity shoot wearing a jacket by a top Danish designer and walked a runway set up to show off the long bar.

I was very excited about going to the opening night party because it was in my home town; I felt like a kid again. A girlfriend and I made our way through the crowds and the smoky bar to the staircase at the back leading up to a level where there was a small area with a couple of tables. 'Look at him!' I whispered to my friend. I indicated a well-dressed young man at one of the tables. 'That guy with the long hair and the blue eyes.' He was part of a group but the others deferred to him and he looked comfortable holding court. There was an air of quiet authority about him. Everyone else knew who he was.

My friend looked at me like I was very strange for not recognising the man, but I had been out of the country a while. 'That's Kasper Winding,' she said. Three years older than me, at 23 he was a songwriter and a multi-instrumentalist who had found fame as a teenager in Denmark drumming with a band called Shu-Bi-Dua. He'd made many albums and with his own band, he was one of the hottest things in the country; he'd also written for musical movies and had hits over a number of musical genres. There wasn't much he couldn't do. And here I was getting ready to pass out like a swooning fan in the front row of one of his gigs. But I had to meet him.

My friend and I circled his table in a self-conscious version of a casual stroll. Each time we passed him, we'd smile directly at him like delirious schoolgirls. It was ridiculous. At the last pass he favoured me with a relaxed smile, introduced himself and asked us to join him. I came over all shy in my overwhelming desperation to sit next to this mature young man with his crowd of friends. Kasper was enjoying a post-gig beer and before I knew it, we had been chatting until midnight and the place was closed. We went on to a pizza restaurant at Nyhavn, an old part of Copenhagen by the river.

There the evening opened out. It was like a first date, with me still feeling stupidly shy and awestruck. Kasper was the first of those men I would be drawn to who were not only interesting but also stood out as excellent in their field: he was phenomenally talented. And despite my embarrassment, I always pushed to meet this kind of person – I had done everything I could to make absolutely sure that Kasper noticed me. I knew what I wanted. After the meal we walked back along the river and it was a warm night (for Copenhagen, anyway – probably freezing cold by anyone else's standards). We kissed and it felt good.

We met a couple of days later, before I had to go to New York for a full week that felt more like an eternity. I was in love with Kasper and it already hurt to be apart from him. We both cried when we parted – it felt so intense but we had just met and our passion was only beginning. Anyone watching us would have thought we'd both suffered some bereavement – we wanted one another so badly. I can still remember what he was wearing that day: he was always so well-dressed, with his long hair covering the trendy scarf that everyone had to have at that time. I felt very alone in the hotel in New York, but I was prepared for it so I was surprised when someone knocked at my door on the first day. Which was nothing to my astonishment at opening it to Kasper, smiling at me in the Manhattan hotel room. The guy with the scarf had followed me!

Kasper missed me so much he'd taken the next flight out to be with me for a couple of days. All those thousands of miles! It was an outrageously over-the-top thing to do and the time we spent together in New York was the most romantic I'd ever had. Kasper had lived there before and showed off his local knowledge. He took me to places he'd played and he knew his way around the New York music scene. His acquaintances included The Rolling Stones, soul singer Teddy Pendergrass, jazz guitarist Ray Gomez, disco queen Narada Michael Walden and musicians who'd worked in a studio band called the Brecker Brothers.

I felt secure with Kasper. His outlook was cosmopolitan, our conversations were all about music and he was so different from those people who never seemed to see – much less approve of – anything that happened outside of their neighbourhood in Denmark. Before he even left New York we had somehow decided that I would leave my parents' place and move in with him on my return.

His apartment was spacious and airy. It was beautifully situated, overlooking the *Kongens Have*, or King's Garden, in the heart of Copenhagen. He had furnished it in a welcoming bohemian style. Instantly recognisable as the home of a musician, it was packed with piles of old vinyl and books and quite a contrast to the way I lived. I looked rather out of place at Kasper's with all my designer dresses, which I liked to have packed away neatly in my room. Often Kasper didn't even iron his shirts – but he was wonderfully free and a true creative spirit. The two of us were very different but whatever we both brought to our party just worked. I opened my suitcases in his bedroom and unpacked my carefully folded Gucci dresses; I lay down on sheets which were as creased as anything else in his laundry, but I didn't care – I loved everything about my new home.

It was important to me that we were both independent: we made our own money and we had our own lives. Kasper also thought that it was working because it was only about four months into our relationship that he asked me to marry him. That was him all over, he was a very impulsive sort of guy and I was a girl who listened to her instincts, but this time we both got it very wrong.

Kasper and I really should have got to know each other a bit more, just given ourselves time to enjoy our relationship and let it blossom naturally. Every time I looked at him I felt that frisson bubble up through me and it felt right. I couldn't control those feelings and I didn't try to think it through – or rather, I made an effort not to think about it. I've always had a quiet warning voice in me that tells me to take a step back and consider situations. I was taught the value of rational thought through my upbringing but I always listened to my instincts. When Kasper proposed I leapt up in a second and immediately yelled, 'Yeah! Let's do it!'

We got married in a church in Christianshavn in the oldest part of Copenhagen. It couldn't have been more romantic. It felt like this was going to be forever. My guests were Mum, Dad and Jan, my grandparents, uncle and aunt. Kasper, on the other hand, could have filled the entirety of Christianshavn itself. He had a lot of friends and a huge family, but mostly he stuck with record industry friends and we had a lot of really cool music to accompany our celebrations.

My mum and I found my dress in a tiny little shop and it was extremely simple with little in the way of accessories. Kasper had a very elegant jacket and seeing him there made me so glad I'd agreed despite the speed of our wedding. Back at our apartment my mum and Kasper's family had set out tables of flowers and rather than have the traditional style wedding band, 60 of us danced into the night to the sounds of the Stones, Bowie and Dylan. It was perfect.

I was on my own in a German hotel room. In my hands was a little plastic indicator: it was telling me that my life was about to change forever. I had been married for two months. Already I knew something was up – my periods had always been so regular and I quickly took the test while I was away on work. A lot of young working women would have been horrified by the implications for their career, particularly those involved in physical trades like modelling, but I felt complete happiness come over me. It just didn't seem to be a problem. I looked forward to a peaceful family life: this would be my new focus.

What was hard to hear and went on to become something that has haunted me ever since was that my mother was not so much shocked as devastated by the news of my pregnancy. 'What are you doing?' she asked. 'Oh Gitte...' Mum had done the same thing at my age – exactly the same time, there were 20 years between us. She knew the demands it made on young people. But I couldn't see any reason why I shouldn't go ahead: I wanted to be like my own mum and dad. Perhaps I would yet go back to work in the local library and bakery; that would be fine.

Kasper was a hundred per cent behind me. He had already had a son, Oliver, when he was 16. He was very wise about everything and reassured me that there was nothing to worry about. My pregnancy was part of what we both saw as a healthy relationship. For my part I loved my growing bump and the little bubbles of life I started to feel. I was so excited and constantly questioned my mum about what was going to happen and what I could expect over the next few months.

After six months I developed what the doctors called hypertension and there were worries about the effects of high blood pressure on me as well as the baby. I was in and out of hospital until at last I wasn't allowed to go home at all and I still had two-and-a-half months to go. Already I was feeling such a bond with the baby that the enforced confinement wasn't as bad as it might have been – my memories of that time were of it being overwhelmingly positive. It wasn't easy for someone as energetic as me to stay quiet for so long but somehow I managed to behave myself and Mum basically set up a library in my room. Books and magazines were piled up everywhere and it was only when it came to the actual birth that things got very serious.

As a result of high blood pressure the baby couldn't get through. It just wasn't coming out – its head would start to move but would then go back. I tried for 36 hours before the doctors intervened with instruments in a futile but also extremely painful attempt to get things opened up. They finally had to give me an epidural and make some four cuts before they could get my baby boy out. I'd been having 30-second contractions for almost three days by then and was practically insane in my agony; I'd almost given up by then. My dad had demanded that they do something to get the baby out. It was a very strange sensation, as if I had somehow accepted that this would go on forever.

And then I had this healthy, beautiful boy Julian in my arms after the most horrendous few days of my life. Nothing was wrong with him and it had all been worth every minute. I was terrified that Julian would have suffered some brain trauma but he was fine and he nuzzled at my breast, making contented noises.

Before the birth I dreamed that I would have a girl – I've always wanted one although I went on to have another three boys. Girlfriends with baby girls had given me some of their old clothes and I was going to call her Isabella or

Monique. Now I looked down at Julian and felt over-whelmed with the most intense love I had ever experienced. It was very specific, something quite unlike the love felt for a man, and it made me weep.

It was just as well that I didn't know in those blissful moments that once the stitches came out I was going to feel unbearable pain all over again. Those days were torture as I waited to heal and looked after Julian at the same time. He would feed and I would love it and try not to disturb him while enduring exquisite suffering as the after-effects of the birth repaired themselves. But I had endless stores of love that made up for it and finally I was able to lie down with Julian next to me and we'd fall asleep together. I felt a very strong bond with him from the outset and even when we have been apart, it's always been there. I know a lot of women who don't lie with their babies for fear of somehow rolling over and squashing them – I just think you have reflexes as a mother which won't allow you to do that.

Then an infection developed in my breast which made feeding very difficult, but we both got through it and it helped that I got a handmade bed from my grandmother. She was Jewish and had originally come from Warsaw. My mother transformed the antique Polish curtains from her old house into sheets and the bed was installed in Julian's own area of the apartment. It all looked so pretty and I watched him swaddled in family history and memories. He had become a little bigger and he smiled a satisfied smile back up at me. I had my own clan now and it felt as if nothing could touch us.

And if the phone hadn't rung some three months after

his birth perhaps nothing would have done. In the spring of 1984 I believed that my life was heading in one direction only. I certainly didn't want anything to change, but when something did sneak up on me I would always follow my heart.

CHAPTER 10

RED SONJA

A beautiful summer's day in Copenhagen and a voice from the life I'd left behind in Italy. David from Elite Models in Milan called me in July 1984. 'Hey Gitte, how are you doing? How's Kasper? And Julian? Hope you're well.' The pleasantries left me feeling a bit uncomfortable. I didn't want to get back into that world again and I knew he had to be ringing for a reason. 'There's a casting in town and they want to audition you for the lead role in a Hollywood movie. Are you ready for that?'

It was out of the question. For a start I was a model, not an actress and I was a family girl now. He was fine with that. 'Your choice, but let me know if you change your mind.' My parents and Kasper were impressed that I'd got the call. Kasper, in particular, had great faith in my talent. 'Why not?' was his typically laidback point of view. They thought it could be a good direction as an alternative to university. I began to consider the option seriously: I only needed to take a flight to Milan to give it a try. Within 24 hours I had called David back. 'Okay,' I told him, 'I'll meet the producer.'

I was agitated on the flight to Milan. *What am I doing?* I thought to myself. I felt awkward and wondered how I looked in my jeans and white tank top. As it turned out I was given a costume, along with the 90 or so other hopefuls. I had a Viking outfit with a sword that looked as if it had come from a fancy dress shop and I was given six pages of script to memorise in 40 minutes.

I had no idea how to approach an audition and couldn't decide whether to be angry with myself for having put myself in such an odd situation with all these girls I'd never met or simply to laugh hysterically. I took a couple of minutes to calm down while donning the funky warrior outfit and realised that, despite the pressure, I didn't have time to learn that much dialogue. *Just do what you can*, I thought. That helped a bit, but I felt so unprepared. I had the ridiculous costume on but I still felt naked. The giraffe in Viking's clothing. What the hell – I could be on a plane heading back home to my family within two hours.

We were told the film was to be called *Red Sonja*, an adaptation of a comic published by Marvel. I'd never heard of either name so that didn't help me at all. The whole atmosphere of the casting was completely different to anything I'd experienced as a model. I'd been to thousands of calls but here the girls were far more competitive. Everyone wanted that lead role so badly; you could smell the jealousy. Where hopeful models chatted with their rivals, even shared an apartment with them, it was all very bitchy here, very cold. It was quite funny in a way because it wasn't my world and I knew I wouldn't see any of them again. The sooner I could get out of that stupid costume, the better: this really wasn't me.

When my name was finally called out I was introduced to director, Richard Fleischer, who was sitting with two other men behind a long table. 'Please, go ahead,' he said. I gave them my most open and honest Danish smile and told them I couldn't remember anything of their script, not one word: 'I'm not an actress, I'm so sorry.' About the only thing I could do was raise the sword aloft – so I did that.

'Stop, stop, stop,' said Richard. 'Okay, don't worry about the script, we'll coach you through what we need you to do.' He asked me to look as if I were really happy. Then I was to look confused – no problem there. Seductive was also pretty easy. I had to follow that by looking as if I was about to give up on everything and saving the hardest for last, I had to cry on request. Somehow I managed it all, though there was some laughter in the crying.

'Thank you very much,' said Richard in time-honoured directorial fashion. 'We'll be in touch.' I felt very silly as I trudged out in my Viking gear. *What the fuck am I doing here? That director must have thought I was a moron*, I thought. I convinced myself that I had never wanted to be in a movie anyway.

I was in the dressing room when a plump little Italian woman summoned me back – 'Mr Fleischer wants to see you.'

The film's producer was the legendary Dino De Laurentiis and he was in his office with Richard when I arrived. There was a desk with two sets of papers. De Laurentiis was a small man with a deep voice and a dominating presence. I seized the opportunity to drop the very few random Italian words I knew.

'You speak Italian?' he said. I laughed and told him I'd picked up some while modelling. 'You did very well,' he continued. 'There's the script and the contract. The part is yours. Whaddya want to do?' There was a pause in which his words failed to sink in. This was like a Hollywood film in itself and I really couldn't believe it.

So what I said was what I always said when faced with great moments in my life. 'I don't know – I'm not an actress. I'll have to phone my dad.' Unfazed, De Laurentiis turned the telephone on the desk to face me and slid it my way.

'Hi Dad,' I said and told him what I'd been offered.

'Well... what do you want to do?'

'I don't know, Dad. They say I'm very good.'

'Why don't you go for it?'

We ended up agreeing that my dad would look over the paperwork for me. The director added that I would be starring opposite Arnold Schwarzenegger, a name which meant absolutely nothing to me: 'The guy with the muscles.' I said that it still didn't sound familiar and anyway I don't like big muscles. They laughed at me, the Danish backwoods girl, and it was all rather embarrassing. Arnold had already made *The Terminator* and *Conan the Barbarian*, though he was still known as the bodybuilding superstar – I really should have had some idea of who he was.

Filming was to begin at the end of September in and around Rome and was preceded by stunt training in London. I did riding – which I already knew well – and how to fight on horseback. I did my own stunts, including falling off a horse properly. For two months I lived in an apartment in London and trained on The Armstrong Farm outside London and with a Japanese fight specialist. Slowly I became Red Sonja. I was totally dedicated to the role and as always, completely professional in my work.

Leaving Julian was hard. I'd just stopped breastfeeding him before I came over and that process was tough enough. Now I had to go away, but when training began he came over with my mum; Kasper too. I was very busy but he shared my excitement at my new role. Shooting was to take seven months and I combined this with taking care of the baby with the help of my family, but I could have done with just another couple of months of being with Julian full-time. The adjustment was one more major thing to take on when there was so much else to learn. Evenings were often spent with a language coach, who helped me turn a very heavy Danish accent into something that could pass for the speech of warrior Sonja.

The trainers were very impressed with how much I already knew about horses and how quickly I took to the physical side of things, choreographing the fighting and the sword play. I would go on to do my own stunts for years to come almost as if I had become a real Viking. Just four months since giving birth and I had become very strong. I threw myself into discovering who Sonja was and learning the dialogue. It came very easily to me and I fell in love with her. She had two sides – the fearsome superhero you see at first and the sweet, intelligent and fair woman you get to know after a while.

Fantasy characters present particular difficulties for an actor in constructing a framework for their role and bringing it out of the realm of the cartoon, but the more I got to know Sonja, I found a mirror for aspects of myself as a woman. Having a baby made it easier for me to identify with her and how she had to balance love with power; the private with the public – that was really what it was all about for me.

Red Sonja saw me typecast as the emotionless super-villain character and that was just too bad. I guess my height and those icy Scandinavian features made it inevitable, but I always look back on Sonja herself, even though she was just a fantasy character, with great fondness and warmth: it was a good time. I was proud of what I'd created in that training period in London and ready to take on the shooting when the production got up to speed in Rome.

Being on set was a great experience. The crew had a way of working which suited me perfectly. I could see how this could become a passion for me in a way which modelling never was. There was a magic to movie making which was meant for me. I was encouraged to create character and express feeling where as a model I was only ever told to be blank-faced. Looking pretty and having a good body were just physical attributes that I only had limited control over. On set none of that mattered if I couldn't turn in a convincing performance – there was so much more creativity.

Even when the cameras weren't rolling I wasn't just Gitte. Everyone called me 'Miss Nielsen'. I was a star! One assistant would be manning the coffee machine, another tasked with making sure I had enough to eat. The attention alone was pretty cool and the life more than made up for the poor pay. I got just $15,000 for seven months work, nothing compared to the sort of fee I could command as a model and probably less than the multi-million dollar production would spend on a secretary, but it didn't matter: I was learning so much and having so much fun I would have done it for free. Everyone had to pull together as a team to make it work – from the director down to the guy sweeping the set. We all needed to make a huge effort to ensure the film happened and I loved that.

I soon learned the movie-making expression 'hurry up and wait'. Indeed, I spent most of my time hanging around for that moment when I would be deposited in front of the cameras and everyone would be ready. In that precise second everything would be silent and as the scene started I had to remember all the lines, all the moves – and to bring them to life. Sometimes there were explosions going off and the set would be filled with fighting and fire but I still had to concentrate on my small section. It took a lot of getting used to but I felt I was coming home and at 21, I knew this was what I wanted to do. I still love that feeling and always have done, whatever film I've been on.

On a set there's always a sense of barely contained chaos and insanity; directors often work themselves into a fury making their ideas work. Everyone on set forms such intense relationships over the course of shooting and the sheer volume of different people working on individual tasks makes every day a constant turmoil of creativity. And then somehow it works out at the end – it *has* to work out.

I soaked up the atmosphere and when shooting finished, I was very quiet and usually returned to my apartment. I lived near the coast outside Rome and Kasper and Julian stayed with me for a while, but it just wasn't practical with me working long hours and six-day weeks, and so they just ended up hanging around for no real reason. Julian was too small to have such constant upheaval in his young life and back home Kasper could get on with his music.

We took turns to visit and when we weren't together I called every evening to find out how everyone was doing, but something had changed. The days with Sonja seemed to be longer and my conversations with Kasper shorter; we talked without actually saying anything. While we never failed to discuss how Julian was doing, we gradually stopped finding out how the two of us were doing. Before long we weren't saying 'I love you'. Our chats were those of close friends, respectful but increasingly distant. Passion had been replaced by trust and routine; there was no longer any chemistry. It was quite a shock for me to realise that I couldn't love him as I had and this was heartbreaking: I had been so sure that my feelings could withstand anything. As the months on location went by, I became increasingly upset about my personal situation – it was clear that we couldn't go on.

It was mostly my fault. As things became more difficult with Kasper, I began spending more time with Arnold. Today, with the distance of time, I can see the tension stretched between life on a movie set and a home life hundreds of miles away but I wasn't capable of managing the situations simultaneously and so I chose the nearest one. I thought that I had a big opportunity to make it in this new world and I gave it everything; there was nothing left of my creativity after working on dialogue, costumes and in the acting itself. I didn't leave enough to maintain a relationship, let alone a family. Always tired, I didn't have the wisdom to balance out the personal and the professional. When I was with Kasper and Julian I did really want to be with them, but there didn't seem to be a workable compromise. My young head was filled with dreams I'd had since I was a kid, and so I went for it.

The crew had become a 143-strong 'family'. Groups of us would go out after our 16-hour days and Arnold sometimes came along. I was naturally very flirty and maybe there was already something there because of our roles in the movie, I don't know: we were supposed to be in love on screen. Away from the cameras, superstar Arnold was charming, kind and confident in himself. Very down-to-earth, though his body always seemed impossible – you couldn't ignore it when we were running around half-naked in our battle gear! He was so out of proportion, it was crazy. I can't say that the look did much for me but he was an incredible sight.

The two of us had energy between us, not only as actors but also as two real people. What started as fictional characters became part of us. It was also hardly news in Hollywood that two people working in the charged atmosphere of a film set might get into some inappropriate situation; that was the way it was. You could be briefly thrown together with someone you found attractive and then, unfortunately, you had to go back to reality. It wasn't any different with Arnold and me.

It started with long conversations about everything and

anything. Work was tiring and the intensity didn't just evaporate as shooting finished. At length it channelled itself into an outrageous affair, and we both knew that when the film was finished, so were we. Time was limited so we didn't hold back – we really made the most of it. The set lights would barely be off before we disappeared to do our thing: we wanted time to ourselves and we wanted to try everything. And when we were alone, that's exactly what we did. Afterwards, I would be back as the rookie actress and he was back to thinking about his dreams, his goal – a long way down the road – of being Governor of California. Even then.

'I love making movies,' he said, 'and I love being an actor. One day I'm going to make it in politics.' I didn't doubt his sincerity or his belief in his own ability, though I have to say I wasn't entirely sure that he would do it, though he was politically engaged: he really wanted to spend his life making things better. He was already world-famous, but it would take years of slogging away in politics to get what he wanted.

'Is that realistic? Don't you think that sounds a little fantastic?' I asked.

'I think anyone can get what they want if they work at it,' he told me with total seriousness, 'if they dedicate their life to it.' When Arnold wanted to convince you of what he was saying he did it in a way that made sure you believed him and actually I was not that surprised when he did go on to do exactly what he said he would. Both he and Ronald Reagan made bad movies and then had huge success in politics. I'm also sure that when Arnold's done with his Californian work he'll come back and do movies again. He never needs to work again in his life, but I know that acting is a big part of who he is as a person and he won't be able to let it be.

Not surprisingly, I wasn't honest with Kasper about what was going on with Arnold. There was such distance between me and Denmark and though it was the only time I ever did anything like that in my life, I still felt terrible. I already knew the marriage was over but the affair meant there was really no going back. It made sense: if I still loved him I would never have been able to go to bed with someone else at all, much less see them for any length of time. I had a big mess of my own making that I needed to clean up when I got back home and I paid for all the fun we had with a deep sense of guilt: I knew that at the very least I owed it to Kasper to set the record straight and try to work out what we were going to do for the future, for Julian.

Denmark, when summer ends, has a particularly dismal grey about it. I was sitting on the sofa in Kasper's apartment gazing over at him and feeling so sorry for how sad I'd made him. He was trying to take it all in – and he was still very much in love with me. It made me think of all those family and friends who said at the time that we got married too quickly and perhaps we shouldn't have had a child together, and yet I loved Julian more than anything on this earth. He was still the best thing that ever happened to me.

However bad things were for Kasper, he showed incredible strength of character in the way he behaved. He always respected the decision I'd made and for me that was the mark of a true man – by which I mean he didn't get angry or violent. We were able to face the reality of our situation together. There were so many difficult emotions and we tried so hard to figure it all out. I knew it was right, but I was utterly miserable. And, of course, in all of this my biggest worry was what was going to happen with Julian. Kasper worked musician hours – in the studio until 3am regularly and sometimes much later. I travelled a lot and had the next four months of my life mapped out in my contract to do publicity for *Red Sonja*.

As I debated with myself about the best solution I went to my mother to get her advice at length. Every mother knows how difficult it is to be separated from their child for any significant amount of time but looking at it through Julian's eyes, I knew that he needed stability and he could only really have that if he was properly looked after by my parents. I only had two weeks to sort everything out before I had to go on a worldwide tour for the movie. It was so painful but also just as obvious that I couldn't take Julian on such an extended trip. I couldn't subject him to endless flights and nights in hotel rooms. Kasper was based in Denmark but he was always busy and frequently out playing late when he wasn't in the studio. We just weren't the parents that I always wanted for my child. Kasper agreed and it was decided that whenever either of us could, even if it was only for weekends, we would have Julian stay with one or other of us, but the rest of the time he would be brought up by his grandparents.

I did feel that this was the right thing to do. In the end Julian spent his first five years with them and I know how much I owe both Kasper and my parents for creating a stable, loving environment for my boy to grow up in. Everything my parents had warned about had happened: I was too young and too busy with my own life to give Julian what he needed. I should have listened, but I followed my heart. I had tried to be responsible and had done everything to have a good pregnancy but when I ultimately needed to step up to the mark, I flunked it.

My parents even suggested I have an abortion when they first heard we were expecting, but I would never have been able to do that. We never regretted it and today Kasper and I are friends, but the falling apart of our relationship was no less painful for our enduring love for Julian. If nothing else, at least we were fortunate in being successful enough to be able to provide financially for our child.

The media attacked me for my decision to leave Kasper and Julian to pursue my own career, but it wasn't just something I decided on a whim. Later still it would be suggested that I had left my husband and child for Sylvester Stallone and it was too good a story for them not to report even though I didn't even meet Sylvester until a long time after my break-up, let alone get together with him. Yes, it was my fault that the relationship failed but it wasn't quite the way it was depicted and it certainly wasn't as casual as many people would like to think.

I not only promoted *Red Sonja* without my first child and my husband but also without my own name. Being told that 'Gitte' sounded ridiculous was not a big deal in relative terms, but changing the identity my parents gave me didn't do anything for my self-esteem at that point. I wasn't Hollywood enough as Gitte, said producer Dino De

Laurentiis. 'What about Brigitte?' he asked me. I guessed I thought it was fine.

Perhaps it would at last let me leave behind my schooldays as Gitte the giraffe. Brigitte the movie star – why not? Gitte was still me but Brigitte was my escape. For me it was more than signing a legal document: Brigitte could be my energetic alter ego in high heels and mini-skirts, taking risks, being provocative and leaping into the unknown. Gitte would always be the home girl, comfortable and informal, who believed in traditional family values and whose goal was to have an ordinary life.

Since the day Dino encouraged me to become Brigitte I have always seen myself as being a woman with those two distinct sides, but they don't always get on. Gitte has always been more forgiving of Brigitte's superficial nature and can laugh off her excesses, whereas Brigitte has less patience with Gitte's shyness and her insistence on following rules. I don't think that the conflict between the two will be resolved, but it's much easier for me to live with both as time goes by.

Brigitte was dominant for much of my career and people always responded to her and she played up to them. It was so much more exciting to be Brigitte – that was when the fun happened. Gitte was hiding inside me all along and I know now that she should have been allowed more space – not listening to her would almost cost me my life. Today I am Gitte first and she is the one who exercises most influence over my work and personal life. You could say that I've only found myself at the age of 47 and that I finally found peace.

It was not always like that.

CHAPTER 11

A COINCIDENCE

Sylvester Stallone was very beautiful. He was the sexiest, most delicious man I'd ever seen. As a 13-year-old I'd seen him in his classic boxer role in *Rocky* while I was a competitive swimmer. I thought the film was romantic and powerful. I'd never been the sort of girl to have posters of movies or boys in my room – I had a picture of my beloved horse instead. Getting autographs didn't do it for me either, but I liked *Rocky* for what it was.

What hadn't made so much of an impression on me when I first saw it was that Sylvester had written the screenplay and had gone to I don't know how many people to try and secure funding. When he finally found someone who was interested they didn't want him to act or direct. As I got to know the movie business I came to realise how much he must have endured to achieve his dreams and how badly he would have been treated along the way. It made me wonder – and still does now – at the self-belief and determination he must have needed to maintain his vision of himself as Rocky in the face of endless rejection. Where did that come from in a man? It got to the point where he was considering using his fee from selling the screenplay to buy his way into the lead role. His was the classic story of battling his way up from nowhere to becoming one of the most successful superstars in the world by the early '80s: it really did only happen in Hollywood.

And here's a tale that sounds like it belongs in the movies – only five days after leaving Denmark for the *Red Sonja* promotional tour I sat down to dinner with Sylvester and his brother. Life was wilder and faster than I'd ever believed.

Arriving in New York I was immediately thrown into the PR machine. I was doing back-to-back interviews from morning until night. Most evenings I called Denmark but I also had friends in the city from my modelling days. We met for drinks but they were accompanied by a very irritating man who wouldn't stop going on about how well he knew Sylvester Stallone. More to shut him up than anything else I said that I would really like to meet the star and if this guy was indeed on such good terms with him then surely it would be easy to set that up.

'I don't have his private number,' admitted our hero. Typical, I thought, that was the end of that conversation. He added, 'But I know what hotel he's at. I can give you the name, if you like.' Now that sounded more like it – I could have some fun even if it came to nothing.

'Girls!' I said teasingly, 'I'm calling Mr Stallone!' I took out a few quarters for the phone in our bar and everyone laughed as I gave the coins a theatrical shake. The very idea of calling up Rocky on a night out was absurd. But I did it – and of course there was no answer. That was an even funnier outcome for us girls in the mood we were in that night, though I did note to myself that the hotel operator didn't hesitate before putting me through. It was clear that Sylvester really was staying there; for whatever reason that thought lodged itself in my scatty brain and wouldn't go away. By the time I got back to my own room that night I had become determined to meet the man for real. How could I make it happen?

I took a sheet of the hotel's headed notepaper. 'Dear Mr Stallone,' I wrote. 'I'm a new actress on my way up and I'm in New York to promote a movie.' I must have sounded like a crazed fan more than anything else. I was excited but I knew it was all too silly. 'I would really like to meet you since I really like your movies. You can contact me in my hotel room at the address below. Best wishes...' I slipped a photograph of me into the envelope and went to sleep. Later some people claimed it was a pornographic image of me – but then some people claimed a lot of things. But it wasn't – it was from the portfolio I used to get work from agencies.

I didn't have a huge amount of money with me and $20 was a lot – but I left the bill with the hotel to ensure the letter was hand-delivered to where he was staying. I'm not sure what I was expecting would happen but I was certainly startled when Sylvester Stallone called me himself in my room. What had just been a bit of a game for the benefit of my girlfriends was now very real and that unmistakeable growl introduced itself through the receiver I clamped to my ear. I was totally freaked out to hear the biggest star in the world talk in person – I felt as awestruck as if I were a shy 13-year-old again and had only just seen him for the first time doing *Rocky*.

At the same time, even though my stomach was churning and I felt very unsure of myself, I knew I really wanted this. It took me back to the time when I was first approached by Marianne Diers in Copenhagen to be a model. I believed that you have to stretch yourself if you want to make your dreams happen and I always pushed myself out of my comfort zone and made myself take risks. If you're not willing to say your desires out loud and go for them then you are left with no alternative but to admit that you've gone as far as you can; it's hard but there's no way around it. I've got so many friends who would make much better stars than me in modelling and acting, but they never got the big role or the Gucci campaign for that reason. Everyone wants to say who they are – but most of the time we are afraid to say it out loud.

Those I've known who have got to the top have talent matched by knowing what they're capable of and the confidence to live like it. You can call it a technique if you like, you can call it whatever you want. The point is that it looks like it works to everyone else – so it does work. Nothing is better for the struggling actor or writer than to be themselves. If you really don't think that you can do it, then you won't be putting in a hundred per cent of the effort that you need to make the leap. That's why so many 20-year-olds end up doing the same thing until the end of their lives, and they may be happy with that, but it won't be for everyone. Inside me is both a romantic dreamer confident that she's good enough and a doubter whispering that it's not okay, that I would be much better off not even trying and I'm cool where I am. Don't try it. Imagine if you try and it goes wrong...

That negative side of oneself is hard to ignore. It has all the excuses – it tells us that there will be a better time to go for it under different circumstances and very persuasively says sorry, it just can't be done at the moment. And so you argue things around until everyone's happy and it seems natural and nothing ever changes. But it's very simple – you do it or you don't; you live it or you don't. Can you deal with yourself or can't you? You may recognise these conflicting energies and battles in yourself – I think we all have them. In me there were always the two Gittes fighting it out – now of course there was Brigitte, which made three of me!

The doubtful side always gets the last word in. It often dictates our lifestyle if we let it. If you're happy with staying where you are, that's fine. Even though I ended up split within myself a lot of the time, I feel positive about having followed what I wanted to do. I didn't play it safe and I didn't allow the paralysis of doubt to overwhelm me. Some people crouch at the starting blocks of a race and see hurdles looming ahead in which they get hopelessly tangled up. Others run a smooth race without focusing on the obstacles and they leap hurdles without even noticing. I would never have got through being a hostage, much less stayed in Paris and gone on to Milan otherwise; I just kept on. The way you approach life doesn't make you any better or worse in the end – it is just a different way of doing things.

As you go forward in life you have a chance to change

direction and you always think whatever you do will be for the best. Sometimes it isn't, but if you're the sort of person who looks to move forward at least you won't be stuck, whatever else happens. If I'd been directed only by the safety represented by my family I would never have left Kasper, but something else pulled me and I had to be completely true to myself. I had no idea what the casting call for *Red Sonja* would lead to, and when I wrote to Sylvester Stallone I didn't know that he would call that night.

My hands shook slightly as I picked the phone up. I answered as Gitte – my new name completely escaped me. 'Thanks for your message,' Sylvester said. 'Let's meet. If it's okay with you, I'll come over in a little while.' I told him it was fine, but I was thinking how crazy the whole situation was: Rocky was coming to my hotel room. *Rocky*! He wasn't even Sylvester in my mind, he was still Rocky. I hadn't thought this far. I looked nothing like the photograph I'd sent him – I was exhausted and I still had Red Sonja's flaming red hair. What a mess!

A friend was with me and we decided on a very simple outfit with a little bit of make-up in the Danish fashion. 'As he comes in – you leave,' I said. That meant I didn't need to get up from the couch to let him in myself and he wouldn't have a chance to see how much taller than him I was.

He was on time and I tried to be as casual as possible. I offered him a glass of wine or water or something – I can't remember. But the topic of conversation we started with was bizarre – divorces. There were 18 years between us but we were both going through the same thing and it made me think that we had so much in common. He seemed to be a real gentleman – sweet, down-to-earth. I was completely floored. I just thought he was amazing. He gave me his home phone number and his secretary's details too, and as he went to leave he said that if I was ever out in Los Angeles, I should definitely get in touch.

I totally forgot that I wasn't going to get up and when he left, I stood to let him out myself. He couldn't hide his shock as I towered over him. I felt rather exposed all of a sudden, looking down on him with my shocking-red hair everywhere – my poise evaporated and I started babbling, 'Oh, it was so nice to meet you, thank you *so* much, it was great, it was lovely… good luck, bye, bye!' And I did this Danish gesture you do with both hands when you're seeing off friends and extended family as if you're excitedly waving miniature flags at them.

He turned as he stepped into the hallway and it was like a movie. 'Red Sonja,' he said, with a very direct look. 'Why don't you come for dinner with me tonight?' Well, yes, thank you, Sylvester. I mean, what was I supposed to say?

'Great. I'll send a car to pick you up in two hours.' With Sylvester went the last shreds of my self-control and I called around friends to share the news. It seemed to me that I was about to go on a date with him and although there was still not much I could do with the Viking warrior hair, at least I had all my experience as a model to draw on to make a knockout impression on him that evening. I had a good choice of evening dresses with me from which I picked out a Gucci and I took much greater care with my make-up.

At 9.30pm sharp the car arrived. Sylvester was at an imposing round table with a tablecloth so white it could make you snow-blind. His brother Frank was there and so was Sylvester's girlfriend and powerful LA entertainment lawyer Jake Bloom, who I had last met in Rome with Arnold Schwarzenegger. It was awkward seeing him again under such different circumstances but Sylvester was quiet and at least Jake wasn't looking at me suspiciously like Sylvester's brother or his girlfriend. I fell on Jake and greeted him as if he was a long-lost best friend.

Sylvester gave the lawyer a look as if to ask how on earth he knew me, but now at least I had someone to talk to in an evening where the girlfriend made it very obvious that she wasn't at all happy with the way things were turning out. I did think it was strange that we weren't there that long before he announced the evening was concluded. There was no natural winding down of the party. 'Let's go, everybody.' Dinner was over. A brief kiss on the cheek and I felt a vague sense of guilt, as if it were me who'd done something wrong.

Well, whatever, I thought, completely nonplussed. Sylvester left in his limo with Frankie and the girlfriend. Jake stayed on for a moment. 'What happened?' I asked him quietly, as if Sylvester might somehow still be listening.

Jake didn't say much before he left. My schedule left little time for me to think things through, though I still wanted to see Sylvester again. I took a chance and phoned to thank him for the dinner. He repeated the invitation he made in the hotel room to call him anytime I was out in LA and I told him that I would.

Flying back to Denmark I thought about his words and something about him made me curious, perhaps fatally so. If I'd been the love-struck fan maybe I wouldn't have done anything more about it and maybe he wouldn't either, but it was more than me being impressed by his style, the undeniably sexy rumble of his voice and the very fact that he made the effort to come and find me. Something more passed between us even in the short time we'd spent together. We'd spoken straight away about personal and painful things like divorce and he had now told me twice to call him up. Single and ready to boogie, I decided I had all the excuse I needed.

Back at home, Sylvester seemed a lot further away than he really was. Everyone, particularly my mother, seemed very impressed that I'd met such a big American star and I guess it was a thrill to talk about it, but as a young, divorced mother living in a small room in my parents' house the chances of ever seeing him again did seem incredibly remote. Work came up all over the world and it was only a matter of time before some agent or other offered me something in America, but I needed a really good plan if I wanted to ensure I'd end up on the other end of the phone with Sylvester in Los Angeles.

Playboy. I'd worked with the legendary photographer Helmut Newton and called up the magazine in my brightest, most optimistic voice to introduce myself. It was always more than a top-shelf publication and for a long time had a reputation for good journalism and photoshoots with the likes of Annie Leibovitz and Marilyn Monroe. Besides, being Scandinavian, I didn't mind doing arty nudes. I'd just finished a movie, I told them. I'd done shoots with Helmut and I would really like to do something for *Playboy*. What I really wanted, of course, was a first-class ticket to Los

Angeles and to be able to say I was staying at the prestigious Beverly Hills Hotel – immortalised by The Eagles in 'Hotel California' – when I called Sylvester. I figured I had a much better chance of making him listen to me if we were both working in the same world.

The deal worked almost too well. *Playboy* also gave me use of a limo for a week and offered me a fee. I had been so wrapped up in promotion and with everything in my personal life that I hadn't noticed *Red Sonja* making me as hot as I thought I had to pretend I was, but I was Arnold Schwarzenegger's co-star: I was big news.

I felt much more confident flying back to America: I was going to leave all the trouble behind me and things were really going to move. So I checked in, carefully took out the piece of paper that Sylvester had given me and phoned his office (it seemed cooler than trying him at home). 'This is Brigitte Nielsen,' I said, using my new name and sounding as neutral as I could. 'I just wanted to let Mr Stallone know that I'm in town and I can be reached at the Beverly Hills Hotel.' It was all so contrived, and the funniest thing about it was that I really did feel rather good saying it – I did feel as if I had properly arrived. Sylvester came on the line and was very friendly. He wanted to know what I was doing and I told him a photoshoot – he didn't need to know it was for *Playboy*.

'Would you like to meet for dinner tonight?'

There was only so much cool I could play. 'Yeah!' I said enthusiastically. 'I would really like to.' I stayed in control that whole week. Every day I would slide into my limo to meet Sylvester, we'd go to a club, his brother might show up, and later Sylvester would try to persuade me into bed but I would gently steer him away from the subject. It was all very flirty and I loved it. We were just playing and although he was persistent, it was always with a sense of fun. Not only was he attractive and in fine physical shape but he was smart and talented too. So many things came across in just the right way: I understood why the world had fallen in love with him.

He showed off a great singing voice and could do unexpectedly funny impressions of famous friends. It was an informal side to him which wasn't always quite so readily on show. I got to see his house and was shocked by how many staff he had – there was security, cooks, plus people working on administration. It was quite impressive and at the same time rather intimidating: it made me enjoy the charm of the Beverly Hills Hotel all the more, with its immaculate gardens and the sense of all the musicians and writers who have been equally captivated by it.

Playboy did the photoshoot in the hotel itself and their crew were as professional as I could have hoped. I had enough experience in front of the cameras for it not to be such a big deal that I was distracted from my main purpose in LA, but I was very proud of the shots I got in those sessions – still am. We even used one of my own outfits, a sort of riff on bondage, which I had found while out shopping with a friend. Chains hung from metal rings attached to little strips of leather and that was about all there was to it. It was great fun and left me with loads of time to spend with Sylvester.

I ran into Grace Jones one night. We'd just finished dinner and Sylvester wasn't in a dancing mood. There was a dance floor as well as a restaurant in this place and needless to say, I was always up for a party. The reluctant Sylvester and I walked over to be greeted by Grace at her terrifying peak and she remembered me instantly from my modelling days.

'Gitte!' she yelled, but with her trademark snarl she made it sound more like a roar. Lots of teeth. Her hands clawed the air as she rushed me. I was wearing a thigh-length, white, cotton-stretch dress with a yellow plastic buckle. As Grace reached me she dropped to her knees and by way of greeting, jokingly buried her face in my crotch. Nice to see you too, Grace.

She stood up to leave a Turin shroud-style impression of herself in all her angular glory imprinted at the intimate heart of my beautiful dress. I could hear a shocked Sylvester by my side take a sharp breath, but I hadn't spent years as a model without always being prepared for a wardrobe malfunction and simply folded and rolled up the long dress to make an unblemished mini-skirt. For his part, Sylvester seemed embarrassed, perhaps understandably. The dance floor had always been my turf but now it made me feel awkward too.

I had given the moment in the sunshine of Los Angeles my very best shot. The spell was broken at the end of my week when I turned back into an ordinary girl on her way home to Denmark. The limo went back, I handed over the key to my lovely room and returned to my parents' house to wait for the next job.

CHAPTER 12

BEVERLY HILLS COP II

I was prepared for the routine of life in my parents' house and I knew it didn't matter that I had a career and a child of my own. My dad's strict rules were still in force: dinner at 6pm exactly, no calls after 9pm. When the phone rang at 11pm my stomach gave a lurch and I ran out into the hallway, but I was too late. To my horror Dad had got there first. 'Nielsen household. How can I help?' he said unhelpfully.

He had switched to speaking English, which meant it must be for me. Dad was still talking sternly and I felt like a naughty teenager. 'I don't know if I can do that for you,' he said. As an international engineer he spoke very good business English. 'However, you can call back tomorrow at 6 o'clock our time. We'll be happy to talk to you then.' Phone down. I gasped, knowing I'd be in trouble now.

'Dad!' I shouted as I ran over to him. 'I didn't mean... who was it? Who *was* it?'

'That,' said my father, 'was Mr Stallone calling for you.'

'Oh, *Dad*! Please, it's like 10 o'clock in the morning for him!'

'I don't care. He can call back again tomorrow.'

We got into a massive argument. He knew exactly who Sylvester was and that we'd spent time together, but there was no getting around his rules. He just wouldn't fucking give any ground: 'This is the Nielsen family and this is Denmark,' he said.

But Sylvester did call back the next day at 6 o'clock, just as directed by Mr Nielsen, and asked permission to see me. My dad made him explain everything while I watched him on the phone in humiliation – I was to be invited to Sylvester's beach house, I learned, as I crumpled with embarrassment. But maybe it was no bad thing that Dad was showing so much interest: there was something proper and formal about the old-fashioned way I was being courted and I was so excited by the news that it was hard to stay irritated for long.

I was soon packed and got my hair done to look its best. Then, with just a couple of days to go, I developed a really bad case of tonsillitis, but decided that nothing was going to delay my departure. We took off in a snowstorm and were then diverted to Stockholm, where I had to wait three hours. I endured 12 hours to Los Angeles feeling feverish, downing tablets and watching my nose go a particularly unattractive red. My mascara was all over my face and I dreaded meeting Sylvester in this state. I kept popping into the toilet to try and fix myself.

I struggled through customs with my nose practically glowing and my eyes streaming, trying to spot Sylvester. After all that he wasn't there – but I supposed I should have guessed: a superstar can hardly be seen to be hanging around the arrivals hall. I don't know what I was thinking. I had imagined it would be like at home when half the family would come out to greet travelling friends with smiles and that funny little Danish flag-waving gesture thing I mentioned earlier. The bodyguard with my name on a sign looked very unlikely to jump up and down waving enthusiastically. This was Bruce, Sylvester's man, and he was tasked with picking me up.

It was a bit of an anti-climax and I rather sheepishly thanked him while thinking that at least I had a bit of driving time to sort myself out. I guessed we would be going by limo and I had become quite used to them – but I had never seen the Mercedes-Benz beast that was waiting for us outside. It was gigantic. And even bigger when I realised with disappointment that Sylvester wasn't behind the tinted windows: the inside of the car could have comfortably served as a family-sized living room. I asked Bruce where his boss was and he gave me a look as if to tell me that I was completely stupid even to think that he might have come to get me.

'He's waiting for you at the beach house,' he said, and I had a beautiful ride along the Pacific Coast Highway to Broad Beach in Malibu. We were greeted by a butler and, at last, Sylvester. I forgot everything as soon as I saw him again and we fell into each other's arms, me apologising all the while for being so sick. We spent a relaxed evening together and the next day I got to swim in the sea and at last I began to feel a little bit better.

That night we were together for the first time. We did it

on a chair – a big, American chair. My main memory of it was that it had finally happened. You know, it was supposed to happen when we spent time together during that *Playboy* week. It was always going to happen. I guess it didn't matter if it was in a bed or on a chair, but I do remember that it just didn't feel right. It was just…weird.

The next morning, Sunday, we had brunch together and later that afternoon Sylvester very directly asked me where I was going. There was a brief silence.

'Excuse me?' I said. Only a few days had passed since he had that conversation with my dad on the phone. He knew I was only in LA to visit him; that was why I'd flown all the way from Europe!

'Well, you know, I've got things to do. I just want to know what you're up to so I can get my car to take you there.' I tried to keep my composure enough to answer him. Then I needed to find somewhere to go. I had a couple of names of agents I knew well enough to ask for help and I was totally honest with them when I called from Sylvester's.

'I came to see him and now I'm here,' I said. 'Pick me up, please, do something…' I felt stranded but by the Monday I was going around LA looking for apartments to rent. I had decided to stay anyway. I didn't have a driver's licence and relied on taxis and bicycles in a town where nobody cycles and nobody walks. I should be in the *Guinness Book of Records* for being the only person ever to cycle from Robertson Boulevard down Sunset Boulevard all the way to Pacific Palisades. It just wasn't done and it was hard work, but I found a lovely little place that fitted my budget and was owned by the great character actor Armand Assante.

That made me feel a bit Hollywood already and I called home in better spirits.

'Dad, I'm not coming back. I'm going to give it a go here – I've got an agent and I'm going to see what happens.'

'Okay,' he said, 'but you'll let me know you're all right.' Then he asked me: 'How are things going with Sylvester?' I lied that everything was absolutely great and said truthfully that I'd paid three months in advance on my apartment. That was showing some faith on my part. I must have something of the Viking in me – I was really determined to make it work on my own terms. I didn't tell my dad that I found it hard to be alone there, particularly at night.

Sylvester called and I was very cold as I said I'd found somewhere and I was doing okay. He sounded very unimpressed, but he phoned a lot and kept asking me down to his place. And again I went. I guess there was still something there between us. We started seeing one another and within just a few weeks he offered me a part in *Rocky IV*. I wanted to go through the usual audition but he took that as questioning his talent-spotting ability. 'Well, if you're really so sure…' I said. 'Yes, that would be great.' But in some respects I don't think I really had a choice. For Sylvester I think me being in his film was part of what it meant for me to be in a relationship with him.

Eventually he did say, 'Can I apologise to you? I'm really sorry. I know you've waited two months but can you pack up your suitcases again and move in with me?' He was very cute and extremely convincing and so I agreed. Apart from anything else it was a pain in the ass living where I was and having to cycle everywhere and he was, after all, not any less attractive than when I'd first turned up. Maybe something would happen. And it did – that was when the shit really hit the fan...

Sylvester's villa was the biggest and most beautiful in the Pacific Palisades. One evening he produced a ring and asked me to marry him. I wasn't yet even divorced from Kasper and I wasn't sure that I wanted to think about it again. Being with Sylvester also meant facing hostility from his inner circle which talk of marriage would only intensify. There were powerful people around him who freaked out at how in love with me he was. He listened to me and they felt threatened by this crazy 21-year-old. They told him that I'd come to steal his money and ruin his life. And for my part, nobody in my family thought it was a good idea.

But the ring was physical proof that he wasn't taking the warnings seriously and it overcame many of my doubts. He must really love me for myself, I thought. If it felt like things were going too fast that didn't matter because we couldn't do anything until I got divorced from Kasper. We got engaged – that was new for me as there's no tradition of engagements in Denmark – and Sylvester's lawyers moved quickly. Within a couple of months the divorce from Kasper was rushed through and Sylvester went down on one knee to propose. I was 22, he was 39. I felt it was too soon to put my career on hold.

But then Sylvester was pulling my hand towards him gently and pressing his head against it, with his mouth doing that famous downwards lip curl. He mumbled his love like a contented bulldog and he called me 'Gitte', which got to me.

That was really me, he knew I wasn't Brigitte. 'I want to marry you and create a beautiful family,' he told me.

I said, 'Yes' – I really did say, 'Yes'. But in a way, the age gap and the doubters had brought us even closer.

That spring of 1985 we settled on 15 December as our date. His mother wasn't invited – although my parents were – but I'm not allowed to talk about the reasons behind that decision here. I can say that was at least partly why I was so startled when Jackie Stallone turned up on *Celebrity Big Brother* to deliver her now infamous battle cry – 'Yeah… Jackie!'

I settled into life by the ocean with Sylvester. Our neighbours included Steven Spielberg and Quincy Jones, who became a good friend of mine. I also got to know Michael Jackson after he came over for lunch. People always seem interested in the big names who lived nearby and it was true that we knew people who were famous all over the world – Aaron Spelling, Bill Cosby, Whoopi Goldberg, Kurt Russell and Goldie Hawn. She was another I'd gossip with and we hung out together. Sylvester and I enjoyed a busy social life and there were a lot of good times.

My parents came over before the wedding for three weeks and Sylvester treated them impeccably. He gave them a beach house and made sure everyone was quiet around them. In every respect he was the model Italian son-in-law. My parents were totally won over and saw the impending marriage in a completely different light.

Film producer Irwin Winkler held the wedding at his house, a complex so gigantic that you might mistake it for a small city. The Sylvester connection was that he and partner Robert Chartoff produced five of the *Rocky* movies, but they were also producers on *Raging Bull* and *Goodfellas*, and Irwin was later to get his own star in the Hollywood Hall of Fame. Even back in 1985 he was one of the most influential men in Hollywood.

The guest list ran to 300, of whom I knew personally a grand total of five – my parents, brother, my personal assistant Kelly and my good, gay friend and stylist Bruce. I recognised most of the other people only from the movies. Under a grand canopy I said, 'Yes' to Sylvester and then people started to come over – John Travolta, Donna Summer, country and western singer Lee Greenwood and countless others. Too many to list, even if I could remember them all.

And the strange thing is that I can't.

When I came to write this book I realised that there were certain memories I always thought were stored away somewhere but the detail had actually gone. It was shocking to discover my marriage to Sylvester was one of those occasions. I can remember up to being in the limo wearing a red cotton dress and no make-up. I was dropped off at the venue and made my way to the dressing area, where Kelly and Bruce greeted me. They started to help me get ready and the next thing I can recall are flowers around Sylvester and I as we held hands and said our vows – and that's it. It feels very strange knowing that much of that whole day has gone. I had to call my mother to ask her who was there and what happened. My doctor has a theory about it: he reckons that because things went so badly wrong with the marriage to Sylvester I ended up blocking out certain events from my mind.

I do remember my dress, because I designed it myself and it was made by Sylvester's own tailor, Charles Bronson (not *that* Charles Bronson). I took inspiration from the 1940s to come up with a simple, white dress with puffed sleeves. That's the only clear picture I have. The guests are indistinct in my mind now, though I do recall thinking that Sylvester's mother should have been there. It was hard for him to come to the decision not to ask her but they didn't have an easy relationship and she didn't like me at all. She never warmed to me even after the wedding.

The press also took against me and decided I was only with Sylvester for his money. Stories suggested that I took tens of millions from him in the end. I don't know where those tales came from – and they still get printed every now and then – or what the purpose of rubbishing me was. I signed an agreement when I married Sylvester which severely restricted what I could say or do but someone must have felt that I represented a big enough threat to warrant wrecking my image. Despite the pre-nuptial agreement, people in his inner circle were still warning him against me on the very morning of the ceremony.

After we were married things began to change. Sylvester was in love with me, but it was very intense. There were pictures of me all over his house – he even had statues made. It was uncomfortable and quite intimidating to see my face looking back at me everywhere I went. When he had a crystal table flown in and had my profile carved into it I began to feel seriously worried. I also felt there was something missing despite these grand gestures and our opulent lifestyle, or perhaps because of them.

We never seemed to get to use any of the riches around us. I remember he had a fully-loaded tour bus. It had bedrooms and a kitchen and with a thrill of excitement I imagined us doing a luxury camping trip – it could be like the holidays I'd had as a kid, except this would be five-star all the way. 'Let's take the bus to Mexico!' I said, my eyes wide with excitement. 'Let's have some fun!' Sylvester laughed and readily agreed, but it never actually happened. There was always some deal to do or some work coming up.

What's the point, I wondered, of money, beautiful furniture, staff and total security if you never stop to enjoy it all? I felt my true self was being stifled. The only time we were ever alone was when we were in bed. There was always someone else there with something that needed to be done. Doing anything spontaneously – or even just hanging out, doing nothing at all – was out of the question. Everyone around him made me feel like he was still single.

A normal day for Sylvester and me would start around 7am. Already he would have been up for two hours, writing in his office. He was a great writer and he had a natural talent for buying the rights to adapt really good books and stories. His creativity and intelligence shone through in everything he did and when he'd finished his first burst of the day we would have breakfast together. We both had fresh orange juice and Sylvester would eat raw fish and knock back a glass of vitamin pills.

I was at least partly drawn into his obsession for healthy living – I'd never eaten less salt or sugar before. As a committed smoker it was harder for me to cut that down but I got by on no more than three cigarettes a week. Of course, that could have been a positive way to live, but the effect was to contribute to an atmosphere between us that I can only describe as sterile.

After breakfast it would be straight to the gym. Some people go to church every day, for Sylvester it was the gym. I would go along as well though such dedication was sometimes very annoying, but it was probably a really good thing for me – I hadn't done much regular exercise since I'd been a competitive swimmer as a kid and I hadn't paid a great deal of attention to myself since I stopped modelling. It was so good for my overall tone and muscles – I'm sure that's why I didn't develop cellulite until I was in my late 30s. The constant exercise helped me to become much stronger and I learned a lot about how to look after myself.

At 9am Sylvester would disappear back into his office. I was left with my assistant Kelly and we'd go off to do dance classes, then shopping and lunch. We would try to have fun, but it was hard when bodyguards were dispatched to watch over us at all times. I wasn't sure what harm two girls could come to on a lunch date and Kelly would always try and get a table where they couldn't overhear us.

In the afternoon we'd come back to the villa, where we'd chat or I'd indulge my life-long passion for jigsaw puzzles. We were just being silly young girls. Kelly headed off around 6pm and I'd get ready for dinner. When it was just Sylvester and me, we would eat as healthily as we did in the morning. More usually there would be a business dinner to attend – lawyers to discuss the rights to some new project or agents to talk about upcoming films. I always found those meetings very boring. When we did go out it would be public – movie premieres, gallery openings or some major event like the Oscars. And when you're that visible all the time you feel like you always have to be dressed up, you always have to play to the cameras.

For a while the constant round of parties and the opportunity to play at being the beaming film star on the arm of Rocky was fun, though in reality there were more business people around than there were creative spirits. Strict protocol was followed whenever we went out. It was a secret order of rules and regulations I'd never known existed before and this Danish Viking was not used to such crippling formality. At least being seen out together would make the world understand we were for real; that's what I hoped. Of course, it didn't make any difference for a press which had a better story to run.

Four bodyguards were on duty at all times. While they slept – on the premises – another four would take over. Eight full-time security men in our home. To me all that was just insane. You couldn't even enjoy a relatively straightforward pleasure like going out for a meal – once you'd got dressed up and the bodyguards had been alerted and you'd been transported to wherever it was you were going, you would be exhausted before you'd even looked at a menu. Not only me, either – Sylvester was under pressure all the time.

The other side of marriage was that with the name Mrs Stallone I got to see places and meet people I would never have done otherwise. When I finally went for my driver's licence it was, like my divorce from Kasper, expedited in a way that just doesn't happen for ordinary mortals. I wasn't allowed to do anything for myself. I didn't have much

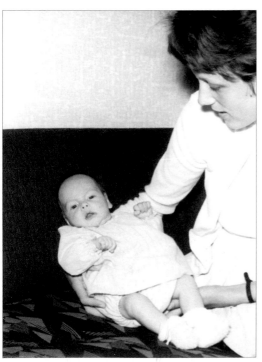

Above: My mother and father, very young and very in love. They are both so beautiful.

Below left: My mother with me at 8 weeks old.

Below right: Me at 2 and a half years old, with my brand new little brother.

Above: My class picture. We all look pretty scary.

Right: July 8th 2006 – the happiest day of my life, getting married to Mattia.

Left: The iconic 1980s shot by Herb Ritts.

© *Herb Ritts*

Above right: Me at nine years old.

Below right: My little brother Jan, my childhood girlfriend Liselotte. Same age as me, but I'm almost a metre taller.

My very first test picture
to become a model.

Gitte Nielsen

Højde 1.79 Str 38-40 Buste 93 Talje 62 Hofte 92 Sko 40½ Hår Mørkeblond Øjne Brune
Height 5'10½ Dress Size 12 Bust 36½ Waist 24½ Hips 36½ Shoes 7½ Hair Dark Blonde Eyes Hazel

Above: My modelling composite that I sent to Sylvester.

Below: First New Year's Eve 2007/08, celebrating with apple cider and Diet Coke.

Above left: Me and my adorable firstborn, Julian.

Above right: Me and my first husband, father of Julian.

Below left: My gorgeous brother Jan, while shooting a commercial for Bacardi rum.

Below right: Me and Arnold in a private moment after a long day on the set of *Red Sonja*.

A happy moment
after a nice dinner
at the old Spago on
Sunset Boulevard.

Above: A great day at Santa Monica beach with my amazing kids – Killian, Douglas and Raoulino.

Below left: My life and my happiness, my husband Mattia and our doggies, Tootsie and Joker.

Below right: Me here in London, having a great time.

money of my own anyway, but Sylvester wouldn't allow me to pay for anything, apart from covering wages for Kelly. Earnings went into an account that he monitored and after a year together he gave me a credit card, which he also got to watch so he knew exactly where the money went. Not that he was miserly – he gave me a limit of $7,000 a month. But what was I going to spend that much on? Nothing was too exclusive, nowhere was too expensive. A lot of things in my life had become very easy.

I appreciated all that and what he did, but what do you do with all of that when you come home and you cry because it doesn't feel like you're somewhere private that you can relax? I told myself that this was my life now. I felt like I was growing up quickly and I learned not to reveal my true self.

Thank God I always had my little brother by my side. Jan never followed rules and refused to know his place; he was just a hippy at heart and had just finished doing a two-year course in construction at university without any clear idea of what he wanted to do next. I encouraged him to follow me out to LA – I missed the fun we had together when we were younger and I badly needed someone I could relax with. Sylvester had been very suspicious of anyone in my orbit. It was different for him with Jan and the three of us got on well together. The atmosphere would lighten for a few hours when we would chat, have drinks and Jan and I were allowed to smoke cigarettes – because Sylvester would be having one of his cigars.

My brother Jan was accepted to the point that Sylvester gave him a job as a chauffeur. For a laidback young guy with time on his hands it was like being paid to have fun. He'd drive the sportscars and mess around with the unbelievably long limousine and I would be cheering him on and laughing like I hadn't done in a long time. And it wasn't as if anyone else was using the vehicles much.

At last I could speak my own language and because so few outside our country knew Danish, Jan and I felt as if we had our own special code. It was a welcome addition to that unique understanding we'd always had anyway. I had a taste of the privacy and freedom that had been missing ever since I moved into the villa: it was like going outside when you've been in a stuffy room for too long. And we behaved badly together – I can tell you that right now. We were a pain in the ass.

Sylvester had a famous game of table football with Jan, who had always been good at it, but Sylvester was convinced he could thrash him. 'I'm the best,' he said, 'but if you beat me, I'll give you the Corvette that's parked in the drive.' Now who does that? Only in Hollywood! And there was Rocky, grunting and breathing heavily with each spin of his plastic team while my brother and I just thought the whole scenario was hilarious. Inevitably, Sylvester lost but he was as good as his word and led my brother out to the drive before handing over the keys to the gleaming, white Chevrolet Corvette to a beaming Jan who, with a contented click of his tongue, graciously accepted his winnings.

I had a 1986 Mercedes-AMG. They only made three of this kind and they were monsters – really, absolute monsters. Now Jan and I could race one another down from the Beverly Hills Hotel to Pacific Palisades. That's quite a ride – the roads all twist and turn. One evening we were interrupted by the sound of a police siren behind us. Oh shit... I pulled level with Jan. 'You've got to go,' I told him. They were right on our tail.

Just before you get to the Pacific Palisades there's a really sharp left turn in a curve going to the right and you just cannot pull through that if you're doing a hundred miles an hour, like Jan was. I managed to get home with my heart racing, not knowing if he was alive. Eventually he appeared – unhurt and even able to fix the car. Sylvester was laughing and it was fine, but I know that Jan and I had been very stupid that night. Young and dumb, yes, yet we were going too far: we no longer had a sense of perspective – everything was provided for us and we had lost our sense of respect.

My brother did look beautiful. We worked out together and he got extensions in his hair so he had a sort of Conan the Barbarian look going on. Jan got himself introduced to Hugh Hefner and would always manage to be invited to parties at the *Playboy* mansion. It was there that he started dating one of the girls. He began to work as a model, starting off on in commercials. One was directed by film-maker Tony Scott in South Africa for Bacardi rum.

Unlike me, Jan was very astute and he saved all his money from this run of success. One day, he announced he'd had enough. 'You know what, sis? I'm a real Dane; at heart I'm just a fisherman,' he said. Like our dad, he loved the peace and solitude of angling. 'This has been fun, but it's not for me. I'm not Hollywood, I can't deal with this. I'm going home.' And so he did. Back home he studied and bought a house. For a while he was so poor he was working three jobs and researching in the evenings. It was tough but he was incredibly determined and focused. Jan didn't become a fisherman, but he did get into eco-friendly energy production. He got into wind farms and is now one of the most successful businessmen in Denmark, doing his bit to combat climate change at the same time. We haven't seen so much of one another in the last few years, but when we get together none of that matters: we're still very close and sing the same old song together. I'll always be proud of my little brother for sticking up for himself – he never let anyone tell him what to do.

CHAPTER 13

A VERY PUBLIC DIVORCE

Sylvester and I signed a pre-nuptial agreement which means that neither of us can say much about our marriage. All I can say is that one early morning in 1987 I took my clothes and jewellery and left his villa for good. I can only underline that it's very difficult to maintain a loving relationship under the scrutiny we faced. A marriage is no place for a crowd and won't flourish if you just live to work: it became a prison for me.

It wasn't just my personal life that was in crisis. My career had stalled too: I had wanted to pursue my passion for acting and I was hot after *Red Sonja*. I had been sent scripts and offered roles, but Sylvester made sure throughout the time we were together that I was busy on his projects. I felt that he didn't want me on a movie with somebody else. Instead I made *Rocky IV* and *Cobra* with him. Even when I got the role as an ice-cold killer in *Beverly Hills Cop II* I knew that Sylvester had a hand in it somewhere. He knew I liked to work but he always had to know what I was doing.

The role was originally male, but it was changed for me. Director Tony Scott thought the part could be made more interesting than the standard villain. I always thought it was something of a set-up – I think the part was rewritten as a favour to Sylvester and the fact that it worked out well was just a bonus. I couldn't think why Sylvester had been okay about that one when he had routinely dismissed other scripts for me out of hand. But however I got there, I felt again that movie-making was for me. Work was again something I looked forward to and I never felt tired when I got up in the morning. It was inspiring to be surrounded by talented actors such as Judge Reinhold, John Aston and of course, Eddie Murphy himself – at his finest. Those were the days of their prime, him and Sylvester! And it was mind-blowing to be directed by Tony Scott.

I got on very well with Eddie. We didn't have an affair, though someone later started that rumour. It was totally wide of the mark. We did laugh a lot and we had a great time. Eddie's a strange guy – when the cameras are off he's shy and surrounded by his people. And because he's not that tall he practically disappears, but when he's on set, he's on fire. You just had to forget about your script because he'd take off in any number of directions. Tony would shout out to me, 'Work with it! Just go with it! Don't stop, just get in there with him.' It was exhilarating trying to keep up with someone so fast and intelligent.

He broke the ice doing the *Playboy* mansion scene. Naked girls were everywhere and all the boys had a tricky time concentrating on their jobs. I just wanted to get the scene over with. Suddenly everyone started laughing and I thought even Tony would be really annoyed – he's a nice guy, but when he's working he's deadly serious. I looked down and Eddie had glued a mirror to one of his shoes and caused hysteria by comically sliding his foot under the girls' little dresses – mine too, grinning as he did a comic double-check of the situation below. He was just so brilliant at dissolving the tensions of life on set. 'You see how you are?' I said, pretending to tell him off. 'And you're supposed to be the star? Forget it!'

When we got to the firing range scene I used a real gun – that's where I got my gun licence and I carried a little .22. I loved those times, different to *Red Sonja* but great to be a part of it. However, I was still aware that I was in some ways in competition with my own husband. I think he was okay with me doing films so long as there wasn't a chance that I would do better than he did. I don't know why he would think that – perhaps to save me, perhaps it was a power thing. I just had the feeling that I wasn't free to do too much.

It was during our marriage that I finally got to realise another dream I'd held for as long as I could remember. A Spanish recording company, WEA International, asked me to record an album. Their stars included Amanda Lear, Bad English, Cheap Trick and The Three Degrees. How exactly I fitted into that roster I wasn't entirely sure – but it didn't matter. They also distributed widely in France and, most importantly, in Italy, where I had become a superstar. The record company thought my name would be good and thought I should do a synth pop single – very '80s. It was the brief vogue that saw Yazoo and the Thompson Twins achieve fame and my attempt would hardly create anything more lasting. All I knew was that the project looked very exciting and it could open up yet another direction for me.

Sylvester was crazy about music. We used to sing together at home and when he was working on a movie he always insisted that he chose the soundtrack. He spent months picking out the right tracks, meeting with artists and repeatedly visiting the studio until he got just the feel he was looking for – he had a natural talent for it. You only have to think of the inspired choice of Survivor's 'Eye of the Tiger' that defined *Rocky III*. Or James Brown's 'Living in America' and 'One Way Street' by Go West.

There was a music room in Sylvester's house which had a karaoke machine. I spent hours in there and when I wasn't accompanying the hits of the moment I'd be improvising. Sometimes my PA Kelly would join in. I am a good singer and performer, but I never took it seriously enough. I do wish I had made myself concentrate on it for at least a year or so, worked harder with my singing coach and taken longer in the studio. I didn't pay any attention to my own critical faculties and even when I was given songs I didn't like, I'd record them anyway.

Every Body Tells A Story came out in 1987 and it was... okay. The album did sell, but it wasn't what it could have been. It didn't work in the US at all, did slightly better in the UK, but it was a hit in Europe. I had a No. 1 in Italy and it did well in Spain and also in South America, but it never took off in the way I thought it should and the fault was purely mine. Still, I got to tour off the back of it in Spain and promoted the album with performances on TV, so although it didn't win me much respect in musical terms I enjoyed wonderful times working with musicians and getting the chance to live the touring lifestyle. Sylvester allowed me to take off to do the promotion and I worked pretty hard to make it a hit, but I was pretty frustrated that I felt I had to have permission to do it from him. That was really what made me realise I couldn't go on living like some kind of robot. I told Kelly and moved out of the villa and into a small apartment and then a hotel, from where I called Sylvester to tell him it was all over. It was the first he'd heard and he went absolutely nuts.

I didn't have a lawyer or an agent and I was basically on the streets. None of my friends would talk to me. For my parents what was hardest to deal with was the coverage of the split when I was on the cover of every newspaper and every magazine.

The public in Denmark had never fallen for Sylvester in the first place. There had been outspoken criticism when we visited that time he saw my parents' house. We flew in by private jet, which normally ensured a smooth and discreet arrival in an airport, but this time there was an anti-Stallone demonstration and someone even managed to break in and spray-paint the entire plane. *That's fucking Denmark, you know?* I remember thinking. I was furious – you might not agree with the man and his views but you don't do that. And I got really angry and defended my husband-to-be in the press. Security was on high alert the whole time we were there.

Now it seemed there was once more no other story. It was widely alleged that I had become a lesbian and that was why we were splitting up. That story was reported everywhere, particularly in the UK, but even in Denmark my father had to endure looks from colleagues who were watching his personal life unfold in their daily paper. The asides and snide questions followed him everywhere and that seemed totally unfair to me. I might have been running with the Hollywood set but my parents really had nothing to do with it. They were bewildered by what was happening to them and the family were angry with me. They had said not to marry him and now it was all a mess; it was all very sad and very ugly. Yet my parents knew that there was no truth in the stories and despite all the shit he was going through my father said to me that if I needed to move back home they would still be there to look after me.

Kelly's family was also hit. I had stayed good friends with her and I knew her family was small but sociable and very religious. They were stunned by the allegations that their daughter and I were lovers and ended up having to move towns. And so it was that two families sustained direct hits in the endless rounds of media attacks. They were split down the middle, with some speaking out in defence and others angry about being caught up in such a personal campaign. I found out that a major PR company had been hired to take us down in a very deliberate way but I never got anything to say who was behind it.

Fox magazine ran a cover story suggesting that I had walked away with $100 million. Other sources put it at just $50 million. Either way I was accused of taking everything from Sylvester and there was nothing I could say. Or rather nobody listened. It was like being run over by a tank. I watched helplessly as my family fell apart and the pain was unbearable, but there was no point in fighting something that was so completely untrue and I realised how little truth there is in most celebrity stories. Even some of my allies came to believe that there was no such thing as smoke without fire, but I can tell you that I've never been a lesbian. Take a look at my track record! I'm not denying that someone can marry and still go on to be lesbian or gay and that's fine, but I'm saying that it wasn't the case for me. I told journalists, 'Just stop it! I'm Danish. The first legalised gay marriage took place in Denmark in 1973. If I was a lesbian, I would say so.' They just ignored me.

Kelly had been my rock throughout the marriage. Because we spent almost every day together there were plenty of photos of the two of us that could be used in evidence against me. I have no idea how these got into the press but it was Kelly I felt particularly sorry for. For almost three years all she had done was be very loyal and she knew everything that went on between Sylvester and me. She would refer to the set-up we had as 'Sylvester's crazy house'.

She and I would take off and drive around Hollywood sometimes, just to escape the place and the bodyguards. My car was fitted with a police siren system – which wasn't, strictly speaking, legal but was one of the perks of being who I was. It could do fire sirens as well and just to give you an idea of how stupid our humour was, I had a tape of someone having a particularly liquid attack of diarrhoea, which we played at full volume down Rodeo Drive, cracking up with laughter the whole way. The genteel ladies of Beverly Hills were treated to thunderclaps of flatulence and we thought it was the coolest thing ever; that tells you how mature we were.

Kelly worked in the shop at Gold Gym, which was where we got talking. Born in New Orleans, she had moved to LA like so many others in search of the American Dream. I was a regular at the gym and I soon got to trust her and asked her if she would be my personal assistant. She needed to be talked around as she'd never done anything like that but she went on to become the best PA I ever had. When I met her she was stuck in a hopeless relationship with a real loser and I think working for me helped her to develop her confidence and move on from him. She organised everything for me and was always there on the movie set and booking tickets for me; she was my shadow in everything I did and she was good at getting things done. There was a tough side to her and she wouldn't take no for an answer. But one thing she wasn't was lesbian; not even a bit bisexual. She has always been passionately, loyally, stupidly in love with men – just as I am.

I had never been after money. My feeling about relationships is that when they're over you've got to get on with your life. I didn't want to get into a protracted battle in the courts which would spin out the divorce; also I wanted to show Sylvester that I was a big girl and I could take care of myself. Everything went really quickly. I took only clothes, a car and jewellery.

A year later I got a cheque for $500,000. Even that was really only symbolic. I'd been told by friends who thought I was crazy to walk away that I could get millions through the lawyers, even after the pre-nuptial agreement, but I found it impossible to imagine fighting a man I was in the middle of leaving. Despite everyone's well-intentioned advice I was determined to start over again.

On 13 July 1987 my new life began as the papers came through without contest. I was only 24 and I had already been through two divorces, I had a child and I had known some of the richest and most successful people in the world – although now I was myself poor.

CHAPTER 14

ITALIAN SUPERSTAR

Offers of work were not exactly plentiful for the lesbian ex-wife of Sylvester Stallone who took him for $100 million. No more movie parts, no more anything; it all dried up. My agent refused to work with me and I never heard from any of those producers and directors who had previously been so keen to work with me. Later, I was told that the word had been passed around that I was not to be hired: I had been blacklisted and at the time I didn't even know.

I became homesick and felt I was being called back to the Old World. It was an exciting time for Europe: the Berlin Wall hadn't yet come down, but young activist Mathias Rust staged his audacious flight over Moscow's Red Square in a little civilian Cessna plane. Music was interesting too. Michael Jackson released *Bad* with the fabulous single 'Man In The Mirror'. If there was one song in the world that I wish I had written, that would be it. He sings about wanting to change the way things are – and if you want to make the world different you have to look deep into your own soul first; you have to face your reflection. That was me – I was ready to change. It was like a message sent to me personally and the words of Michael Jackson gave me strength when I felt very alone.

I was knocked out by the force of the storm. Friends turned their backs on me and I had to reassess a lot of things in my life. A lot of promises turned out to have meant nothing, but I was still healthy. I had my sense of humour, I still had a family – even if they were a long way off – and Kelly was by my side. Most of all I had my beautiful son. I had the important people and they backed me a hundred per cent. When $500,000 landed in my bank account from Sylvester I was even able to buy myself a little house.

Kelly kept me positive. I had got stuck remembering all the good things Sylvester and I had shared and it was her who got me clubbing again in Los Angeles. And although I felt like shit, I still looked great – I was quite awesome at that time. The paparazzi still loved to follow me as I tried to forget Sylvester but at least there was no internet yet, so no YouTube. I was able to retain some kind of a private life.

Hollywood's hottest clubs included a very cool converted fire station hangout of De Niro and Joe Pesci, which we stormed. We partied with Jack Nicholson and George Michael – I have to say, I had *the* best dance with George Michael and I knew he was gay and it was just so sad! In a quiet corner was shy Michael Jackson and he didn't go out dancing despite that onstage persona, but he wasn't withdrawn – you could have a long conversation with him and he was often very funny.

At last an offer of work came and it was from outside the States. An Italian company gave me my first million-dollar contract to co-host a prime-time TV show in Italy. Their viewing figures regularly went above 15 million and could hit 30 million at Christmas. At that point I could speak a little bit of Italian from my days modelling and shooting *Red Sonja*, but I wasn't able to carry a conversation. Even so, there was a great deal of interest in me as the ex-wife of Sylvester Stallone and money was in plentiful supply – it was the height of the '80s. I was ecstatic. *Great!* I thought. *I'm going to show Sylvester I don't need to sue him to get money, I can make my own. People want me and I can do things I really want to do.*

When my plane touched down in Italy it was surreal. It was more like the Beatles or Tina Turner had arrived. I thought I was going to die in the middle of the crowds who had turned out to greet me. That freaked me out because I had hoped that I would have more freedom now I was on my own. The Italians were very physical in their affection and it was a very different kind of attention to what I would get in Germany or the US, but I plunged straight into work and everywhere I went, I was escorted by the police like a politician.

The TV show ran for seven months during which Kelly commuted with me between LA and Rome. I made so much money and I could have had any man I chose: I was at that level of success where nobody cared what I looked like or what sort of person I really was. It was all about fame and that made me feel quite lonely. I was withdrawn outside of the job: most days I would work my butt off and then just go home, turn on the computer, play a game and crash out. Kelly started getting really worried about me. I began to get paranoid about other people. Did anyone want me for who I was? Would they still like me if I was ordinary Gitte or did they want to spend an evening with Brigitte Nielsen?

Kelly told me my fears were just bullshit. 'Get over it – have some fun,' she said and offered an antidote to my solitary life. 'Why don't you go out and get laid?' But I didn't think it was such a good idea and so things went on: I lived my life in the studio and went home to sleep…until I saw an article in a magazine that had been left on set. I flipped through the pages glancing at the Italian until I saw a feature on an American footballer. A huge picture of him dominated the article and it made me remember Kelly's suggestion. I'd never heard of this Mark Gastineau but I said to Kelly, 'Okay, you get in touch with this guy. I want to meet him!'

'But he's back in the States,' she protested. 'You should be looking here.'

'No,' I said. 'This is the guy I want to meet. Get it organised.' According to the article Mark was not only really nice but he grew up in a conventional religious family on a ranch in the wide-open spaces of Arizona. He had been around horses all his life and he wasn't a movie star, he was a sportsman. It was something different that attracted me to him. 'If I can have anyone,' I said, 'then he's the one I want.' And Kelly and I laughed about it – here was the guy who had grown up in a Western saddle on a farm, he had taken part in rodeos when he was 12 and he started playing American football when he was in high school in 1979.

Then the New York Jets signed him on a major contract. I got carried away with the story and latched on to elements from my own upbringing in Denmark, which seemed to be reflected in Mark's early years outdoors. I also saw a powerful man who played sports.

Within a couple of weeks Kelly had arranged for me to meet Mark at the Beverly Hills Hotel when he came to LA to do PR for his team. *Oh my God!* was my first thought on meeting him in my room – he looked like a tank. He was large in both directions, weighing about 130 kilos and measuring almost two metres. I had never seen such a massive individual in my life. Arnold Schwarzenegger and Sylvester were like little boys next to the colossus that was Mark Gastineau. But the thing about Mark which you wouldn't know from looking at him was that he was also fast as a cat, seemingly untroubled by his bulk.

After a couple of drinks and a chat I began to think that maybe I'd made a mistake: there was no fire, no excitement. I didn't feel what I thought I would feel having read that article but that didn't mean we couldn't part on good terms – except that he wouldn't leave. He kept insisting on staying, although it was getting late; he was pushy and it was kind of embarrassing. 'Okay,' I said, 'but you have to sleep on the couch.' It was an uneasy moment – he was famous enough to be insulted by that and anyway, I didn't know him – he could easily overpower me if that's what he wanted, but he respected me and I thought then that was pretty cool of him, though of course, it wasn't at all cool to have refused to leave in the first place.

We kept in contact after that first night for whatever

strange reason: I was over from Italy often enough to catch up with him on a friendly basis. I don't know what it was, but I didn't cut him off completely. Part of me was fascinated by him and intrigued by that astonishing body. I was open to his telephone invitation. 'Come to visit me in Arizona,' he said. 'I'd like to show you where I come from.' Rather wide-eyed, I agreed without thinking about it. It was a plane ride from Los Angeles to Scottsdale and I almost immediately regretted my decision when I arrived at the smallest airport I'd ever seen. It was a little bit spooky.

The place was deserted, the walls were cold and I realised how little I really knew about Mark as I looked around, clutching my small suitcase in one hand. It all felt very strange and where was he? I waited and waited as the few people on the same flight disembarked and then I really was completely alone. The airport was poorly lit and it began to feel like a scary movie: airports feel weird when they're empty.

Angrily I thought to myself, *What the fuck were you doing? You arrive alone, you don't have his number – you're a complete idiot!* Still clutching my suitcase I wandered around the gloomy terminal building looking for a phone. I had a few coins and I thought I would call someone. Anyone. My plan was interrupted by a bloodcurdling scream. Long and loud, it sounded like nothing human. It was a maddened bear about to attack. It was... Mark. Of course – why not? That fucking guy! It was inevitably my Mark – he had decided to freak me out by jumping out at me from some shadowy corner.

I readied myself for a fight and saw a big grin break out over his face.

'Aha!' he said, laughing. 'I've been here all the time – watching you!' Not quite the reassuring words I might have hoped to have heard. He continued, 'But you look *great*!' He sang out 'great' like a delighted child, making the word two syllables. I thought he was nuts. Then he grabbed me – he picked me up bodily.

'Welcome to Arizona!' he roared. 'Beautiful Arizona!' It was like he was delivering the pay-off to some tourist commercial. And with that he started swinging me around. Now, I hadn't even been with a guy who could lift me out of bed – let's face it, I'm a giant woman – and here I was seeing terminal lights blur around me as I was whirled about as if I were a doll, accompanied by Mark's deafening roar. I joined in the racket, screaming for him to put me down. When he did, he took one look at me, one look at my suitcase, took it in one hand and my hand in his other and we walked out of the airport.

I'm not sure what I was expecting by the time we got to the car park but I guess under the normal circumstances, which these certainly weren't, it would be a big old American pick-up truck or maybe a footballer's limo. In front of us was a dented wreck, filthy outside and inside too, and the smell emanating from it was overpowering. I wasn't so bothered about what kind of car it was, but I did think he might have gone, 'Okay, she's coming to visit me...' and have washed it at least. My father had an old Volkswagen, so I wasn't being picky, but at least Dad's was clean inside. Mark was a superstar – it was all just so weird that his car should be like this. Everything about this trip was weird. Maybe Mark was simply a cowboy, a down-to-earth guy. That was what had attracted me in the first place. But now I didn't know any more. I had no idea what the fuck I'd been thinking or how I'd gotten myself into this.

We made our way out of the grimy airport and hit a series of small roads heading deeper into Arizona. Outside Scottsdale and away from Phoenix the tarmac gave way to dirt tracks and we bumped to who knew where. It was pitch-black and I sat nervously by this big bear of a man in his smelly lair in the middle of nowhere. I didn't really know him, did I? And what could I do if the plan was for me to end up in a hole somewhere out in the desert or worse? By now, I was really paranoid and panicky. Forget houses – this guy was as big as a hotel.

I turned in on myself. *You're young, naive, spoiled and dumb*, I realised. Terror gripped me and it took a while to notice that we had come into an area that even in the darkness I could just about make out wasn't too unlike Palm Springs in California. Mark swung off the road and up a long drive then parked in front of a big, beautiful villa. In daylight it would look like Wisteria Lane from *Desperate Housewives*. *All right, Gitte*, I thought, *this might not be so bad*. Mark seemed to have heard my thoughts. 'Aha!' he said, again that teasing laugh. 'We're here, honey! And don't worry because I've got no furniture in the house at all.' Oh, and I had just started to relax. The lights were on in the house... had he recently robbed it or something? But he got out of the car and took out a key for the enormous double wooden doors that reached up to the roof.

Inside there was wood everywhere and thick, cream, wall-to-wall carpet. And, just as he'd said, nothing else. It was a

500-square-metre house – that's a lot of nothing. Our voices echoed emptily up to the high ceilings. I remembered myself breezing through busy Los Angeles airport earlier: I couldn't even get back to Scottsdale when I had no idea how we'd got here in the dark. This was not safe.

'I'm going to have furniture soon,' said Mark unreassuringly, 'but let me show you around.' He dragged me around this enormous, lifeless house. The master bedroom was scariest – it seemed even larger because it contained just two old mattresses slung on the floor. Their presence was worse than if the room had been completely empty. I couldn't take my eyes off them and how they seemed to speak of some horrifying plan. Stupidly, I started to babble away. 'Very nice... so you'll have furniture soon... how lovely...' But the terror was rising in a scene that only lacked the accompaniment of screechy violin stabs to make it complete.

I tried to guide him to any other room, but we ended up back in the bedroom and once more he lifted me bodily and this time he threw me on the mattress. He placed his huge body on top of mine and pulled my head towards him. I thought my last moment had come, but he only whispered in my ear, 'Whatever happens, don't be afraid, but if you are at all frightened... Look up.' It was unbelievable. Look up at *what*? Look straight up... I'd been so transfixed by the mattresses and the ceilings were so high that it was only then that I saw the hundreds of heart-shaped balloons floating way above me, each inscribed with, 'I love you'.

The relief was incredible as tension flowed out of me into laughter. Mark stood up and reached out, jumping to grab one of the balloons by its string. 'This is for you,' he said. 'Don't worry, I am a little crazy but I'm a gentleman – a crazy gentleman.' And he took me for dinner. We ended up having a surprisingly enjoyable evening together. I realised the whole episode had only been about getting to the balloons and he'd wanted to scare me because he thought it was romantic. Was it really that? I didn't know. But I had been right in the first place – he was lovely, yet even so, I thought to myself, I should have known better.

With the sun shining the next morning I could see the area around his place was stunningly beautiful. His horses were nearby and there were quite a few other houses not so far away. Mark explained the house was empty because he had just divorced and his ex had the furniture. For some reason connected with the divorce he didn't have access to his money and all he could use at that point was the house itself and that delightful car which he'd picked me up in. At least it all made sense to me now.

Mark didn't appear to be worried about the situation. He was crazy about being in Arizona and totally relaxed about everything else. For him, it was like – 'Don't have anything... got a house, no furniture, fucked-up car outside and... hey – what's wrong with that?' And I thought, *Yeah! What's wrong with that? If you like the guy, who cares?* It was somehow refreshing when everyone else I knew was obsessed by how much they earned, how much other people earned and how many possessions they had; this was kind of cool. Still, I remained a little nervous of him, but at the same time we seemed to be working out. If you really like

154

someone, it doesn't matter about being taken to a five-star restaurant by limo.

Mark's furniture problem was partly solved by me bringing a bunch of my stuff from LA to his place and we moved in together. I kept my house on but I enjoyed the peace and quiet of Arizona, where I could be free of all the media bullshit. There were no long lenses pointed at us and nobody to check where we were eating and what we were up to. My world began to change. I met football players and all kinds of people who were involved in sport. Once Mark and I took a limo on the playing field when the Jets played the Washington Redskins in 1988. This was hallowed ground and no wife or girlfriend was usually allowed. It was a great game which they won and the press were out in force. And after all the fuss we could sneak off and go back home to Arizona and our down-to-earth lifestyle.

The spontaneity I had lacked in my marriage I found with Mark, who believed that as long as we were happy, everything was okay. We seized each day as it came and life was never boring. He loved nature as much as I did and often we would go into the stunning White Mountains nature reserve or gaze out over deep lakes which were popular with anglers. Mark the bear-man took me to see the genuine article in their habitat and even as I write this, I think I could easily go back and live there again. Summer there was really hot and winter properly cold – all four seasons were vividly defined in the wilderness. Mark's untamed character made sense.

We took off on two-day fishing trips, going out with the dogs and sleeping under canvas. Mark built fires and together we stargazed under blankets, sometimes not even sure of how we would track our way back home the next day. This time away from the spotlight meant everything to me. Seeing the Salt River was amazing too. It made me think of how I used to run away from being bullied at school and now I was escaping limos and finding myself again: I felt at peace and at one with myself. I got myself back into horse riding and that gave me a sense of harmony which I hadn't felt for a long time. And I could always drop back into my working existence when Mark was playing – I flew to Italy or New York but now I knew that I had a sanctuary to come back to. Sometimes during the football season we would go and stay in a house he had in New Jersey.

It was no longer so hectic that I needed someone to organise everything for me so when I moved to Arizona it was without Kelly. She was incredibly upset because she thought that no matter where I went or what I did, we would be together. And I do wish on some level that I'd kept her on with me, but I was in love and I had a new life. I would never have a friend like her again. We met up when I started writing this to talk about the old days and, just as with my brother, it was as if we had never been apart. I do hope that we will have a chance to get together again in the future. She's a Louisiana girl with the big accent to match and a sassy style which I miss terribly. I have to admit that I left her stranded but I was relieved to find when we spoke again that she had become a very successful estate agent in Atlanta. I was really happy for her. At the time I was too wrapped up with Mark to think about much else and thought that I might never leave the desert.

CHAPTER 15

LEAVING ARIZONA

Mark came from a dependable, religious family. I got on well with them, particularly his sister, though I didn't like the way Mark and his father would get drunk and go into Phoenix and sometimes get into fights. They could become like a pair of football hooligans when they would leave me and his sister to go off on their adventures – they had a kind of blood lust as some men just do. Whenever they returned I would try not to imagine what shape their opponents were in. Mark's father wasn't quite the same size as him but he was pretty well-built.

It was a disturbing side of Mark I also saw when he fell out with his neighbour in New Jersey. He battered at their party wall until he actually broke through. The neighbour called the police but no charges were brought. My brother Jan got the full experience when he came to visit and we shared a limo with Mark, who started messing around in the back. Before long he took the whole vehicle apart, from the carpet via the plush seats to the upholstery on the ceiling. Everything went out of the window. Jan and the chauffeur glanced nervously at one another when their eyes weren't glued to Mark ricocheting around the passenger seats like a massive pinball, first wrenching out the mini-bar and gradually working his way up to the television.

When we arrived at the restaurant, Mark calmly stepped out of the car and told the chauffeur not to worry and to send him the bill. We finished our meal to be met by a brand new limo delivered discreetly by the hire company and, surreally, the evening continued as if nothing had happened.

The reason for Mark's increasingly unpredictable behaviour lay in his use of steroids. I should have realised early on when he asked me to pick up what he called his 'vitamins'. I guess I decided not to see what was going on, but I don't know why. I didn't want to accept it until it was too late.

I went for a smear test in New York and it came back that something had shown up. In the follow-up appointment I was told that I had cancer of the uterus. They told me I had to be operated on immediately. I was numb with terror. It had never occurred to me that I might get cancer – I had always been so healthy. How could that happen to me? I was shocked into doing exactly what the doctors said. There was no time to waste. They knew if they didn't act immediately I didn't have a chance and there was no time to respect feelings.

I'd long been seen as indestructible. My reputation as the irrepressible ex-wife of Sylvester Stallone didn't fit with the weakness I felt in radiotherapy. Looking back, I think I probably became depressed – I was always so upset and everything seemed to be going too quickly. My mum was a tremendous source of support. Despite the nine-hour time difference we spoke a lot on the phone, often into what was late night for me. It didn't matter – whenever I needed it, she was there to talk me through the hard times.

Mark asked me to come along to a meeting with his football team boss. This was quite unusual. As a player you weren't expected to bring partners along to discuss work and the management were clearly waiting for an explanation. 'Brigitte has cancer,' Mark said. 'I'm going to have to give up football to look after her back in Arizona. She's going into a clinic and I want to be by her side.' His words made me embarrassed – I had no idea that he was going to end his career for me but it was also uncomfortable to have my illness discussed so publicly. I looked at him. He was doing that for me? This was a real man – he would walk away from everything for me. It made me cry, though there was also something a little strange about it all. Here I was in the man's club and it didn't quite add up when they just agreed straight away. Wouldn't they fight for him? But of course I pushed away any disloyal thoughts and allowed myself to be lost in the romantic gesture.

It was only years later that I discovered the real reason for that meeting. Mark had just been pulled up for the third time in relation to the misuse of steroids – and that meant he wouldn't be able to play for the next three years. At his age it spelled the end of his career.

Without the steadying routine of training and playing Mark's behaviour worsened. What I thought of as his crazy moments were beginning to join up together, though they were still softened by the small, sweet things he would do for me. I knew he had a good heart. He could be very serious and I wasn't so interested in his muscle-bound exterior – it was what was deep inside that I loved: the good, fair guy who was as happy in nature as I was. This was the personality that steroids were working hard to destroy. When he was in their grip, he became an entirely different person.

He had raised his voice at me before and a couple of times he cuffed me with his hand, but I was used to that and it was okay. When he was no longer a professional footballer but still using steroids he became more irrational and actively dangerous. He would shake me and growl, 'I'm going to fucking kill you...' There was always that undercurrent of violence from him but I told myself that it would get better – that's how I kept going.

I got a part in a HBO movie called – ironically, as it turned out – *Murder by Moonlight*. Shooting took place in England, which involved relocating temporarily to London. Mark accompanied me and his jealousy and anxiety meant the crew didn't want him around on set: he was so unpredictable. It was up to me to pass the news on to him and I knew that a bomb was going to go off at some point. The fuse had been lit and it was now just a question of waiting for the inevitable. I couldn't think how to deal with the danger and at the same time keep going with the heavy demands of the job. The detonation came when I least expected it.

In a break from filming I had returned to our room, and

that was when Mark seemed to lose control of his senses. He held me under the water in the bathtub. The water was ice-cold and I could find nothing to grab. Not that it mattered – he was easily strong enough to hold me under the freezing surface. I fought for five or ten seconds, but then I gave up. It was clear that his rational brain had completely switched off – he was blinded by anger and all that remained was that awesome strength. Silently, I gave thanks for my life and hoped that I would be remembered. I hoped Julian would remember me and grow into a good and happy man... I swallowed mouthfuls of choking water so cold I thought its temperature alone would make me pass out. Briefly, Mark pulled me up, perhaps regretting his temper like a small boy caught out, but then he seemed to think better of it and down I went again, so I gave up. I felt a calm, accepting warmth; I felt comfortable, the fear had gone. And then he lifted me out of the water.

For such a violent man, he had a sweet, kind side and I guess that's what I clung to; that was the scariest thing. I forgave him but deep, deep inside I knew I had become more frightened of him than I had been of any human being.

I continued cancer treatment and it was eventually pronounced successful. I'd been told that it reduced the chances of becoming pregnant and so I was completely startled when that's exactly what happened. It must have been something that was meant to be – even my father laughed that I was designed to have children. He would joke that it was enough that someone looked at me to make me pregnant, but it seemed like he wasn't far wrong. I was so happy to have proved the doctors wrong, though I don't know what it was that made me keep the baby and stay with Mark. I knew that the relationship probably couldn't survive and I was feeling yet more sensitive with a child inside me but I still knew that I could never have an abortion.

I believed that Mark did love me, even though steroids had by now totally overwhelmed him. The pills still only rarely showed their face to me but they were there and part of him. And now it wasn't just me that I had to consider, but the baby too. Could I really have a safe and secure relationship with Mark or would I have to think about leaving again? I decided to stay until the child was born and I would be strong enough to make any necessary move. It was a fatal decision.

Baby clothes became my priority when we got to the eighth month and I spent ages in a shop discussing the options with the assistant. Mark was with me the whole time. By the time we got home he was in a black mood. 'Why were you that nice to the guy in the shop?' he shouted. I don't know what he thought he saw but it was only steroids whispering to him. He couldn't really think that a woman just a few weeks away from giving birth would be flirting with someone selling baby gear. But there it was. The row continued as I went on with changing in the walk-in cupboard off the main bedroom.

Nevertheless, on 15 December 1989 I gave birth to a beautiful, healthy boy and just nine weeks later, I made my escape from the desert of Arizona with baby Killian in my arms. My mother, who had come out to visit me earlier with Julian, was completely behind my decision. All she wished for was my happiness – she just wanted me to be strong again. I waited until Mark was out of the house, just as I had done with Sylvester, took a few important items for the baby, gently placed him in his car seat and drove to Los Angeles without a break. All the while I cried helplessly – into the evening and through the night on Highway 10. The sun came up as I was leaving Arizona and I could see it stretching away behind me. It was beautiful and I knew I would never return.

I spent the next three weeks at the Four Seasons Hotel in Los Angeles in terror waiting for Mark to show up. Would he be angry? Would he try and take my son from me? He didn't and apart from one short conversation on the phone a year later, we haven't spoken or seen one another again.

CHAPTER 16

MY TRUE FRIENDS

When you come off your bike you always feel embarrassed. Someone rushes over to help but you brush yourself down and insist you aren't hurt, not really. You wave them away but the reality is you're biting your tongue not to cry and you can feel exactly where you've cut yourself under your clothes and you think you're bleeding. You just hope it doesn't soak through because you don't want anyone you know to see that you've actually been injured. You reckon you look a bit stupid, you're trying to retain your cool, but this is not okay. You're determined to deal with it yourself.

That was what it was like to be in a relationship with a violent man. I felt shame and also a sense of injured pride. I needed to fix things on my own. I'd failed, just as if I'd fallen off my bike in front of everyone. Now I needed to get on with it. But what if having that tumble off your bike gave you concussion? Or internal bleeding? Do you ask for help then?

I never did, but now I know that my determination to deal with Mark on my own meant that with every blow I was saying I was ready to accept another. I lost the ability to distinguish between right and wrong, and my self-respect was ebbing away. I packed my bags countless times in my head but went on taking the abusive behaviour. It became easier, if anything. Now I tell you that I know there is nothing heroic – absolutely nothing – about staying in an abusive relationship. There is nothing to fight for. Not only will it not get better, but it's going to get worse each time you allow it to happen. It's easier for you to sacrifice *your* body and *your* self; it's a very strange pattern. That's what I say when I'm asked why I didn't leave.

Everything has a beginning. There has to be a first punch or kick and that's when you call the police – the first time. No matter who it is, you just have to do it. Or if you can, you have to get in a trusted family member, but if for any reason that's not possible then it has to be the police, straight away. Then you have to get out of that relationship – find a solution. But find it that first time: it will be too exhausting otherwise. You can't stay in a situation that you know, deep down, will only get worse. You may not be able to see the exit clearly, but it will only get harder to find with time. The lightest smack is not okay.

I accepted bullying when I was at school and even though I thought I had left it behind, I was still letting it happen when I was with Mark. It would take another crisis, much worse, before I was finally able to change things for real.

In the immediate aftermath of the split I patched myself up as well as I could. I licked my wounds as you do and I put it all behind me – the desert life, the trips between London and Arizona, the B-movies, C-movies and the parties. The only thing I was sure of now was Killian, my beautiful son.

Killian didn't get to see his father until he was 20. There had never been a birthday card or letter until then – Mark didn't see him grow up and he didn't know that as he became a handsome young man in his own right he kept his father's name (his middle name is Marcus) and that he carried a picture of Mark around in his wallet wherever he went. Like his father, Killian was afflicted with psoriasis – a skin disorder – all over his body. It was tough for Killian but I always tried to speak well of Mark in front of him – it was the least I could do for my son when he was young. His dream was to meet his father one day and I wanted to keep that alive for him. It was only at Christmas last year that I made that happen. And Killian's better for it.

Mark's own life continued to be marked by conflict and violence: he's now in jail for trying to burn a girlfriend. He was still well known in the US as a sporting legend – his record 22 sacks, or tackles, in a single season stood for 17 years and he even tried to make a comeback as a footballer. He's now a born-again Christian. I ended up meeting his ex-wife, Lisa, when she got a reality show called *The Gastineau Girls* and Brittny, the daughter she had with Mark, was also on the programme. I remembered how I sometimes used to look after her when I lived with Mark and saw how she has since grown into a beautiful girl.

I seemed to live most of my life on a plane after leaving Mark, flitting between London, Los Angeles, Italy and

Denmark but I really wanted to settle down and to be closer to my son and the rest of my family. I toured Europe to support my second album *I'm the One... Nobody Else*. This was another WEA album recorded in Los Angeles which did about as well as my debut; not a huge success, but it wasn't a disaster.

I developed a great working relationship with the Austrian rapper Falco, who had a big hit in the UK with 'Rock Me Amadeus'. We performed a duet called 'Body Next to Body', produced by the legendary Giorgio Moroder. The single did brilliantly, hitting No. 1 in Japan, but I still wasn't doing enough about music to make a real success of it.

I still had fun touring though I was always aware that I wasn't developing as a singer, but I got to do shows with both La Toya Jackson and Cher – and I have even recorded a few singles since then. One standout was my 2000 hit, 'No More Turning Back', which I recorded under the pseudonym 'Gitta'. And I also performed a duet with RuPaul, 'You're No Lady'. I was never the best of singers or musicians, but I did enjoy that time.

I began to make the most of my time as a single person and I started seeing Tony Scott, a true Englishman. Brother of fellow director Ridley, he was quite a bit shorter than me, balding and 15 years older. We had made a connection during the making of *Beverly Hills Cop II* and there was an undeniable chemistry despite his physical appearance being so removed from my ideal. We just clicked and we enjoyed one another's company. The romance was right but the timing wasn't. When we first met we were both married but I'd often find that over the years I'd have him on my mind and would think, *What if...? What if we ended up married...?* But it was never quite the right moment and we ended up with something just as valuable – if not more so – as we found ourselves becoming soul mates. Wherever either of us was in the world and whatever we were doing didn't matter: we were always there for each other.

And I'll never quite know why I ended up choosing the wild Mark Gastineau in the desert instead of a sweet, stable, honest man in the shape of Tony Scott. I always say that I never really regret things because I believe that you always learn something but when it comes to getting together with Tony, I do make an exception.

Another of my great soul mates came in the rather unlikely form of a small, dark-haired, blue-blooded Hungarian countess. Eva sat next to me at a girls' lunch hosted by model-and-actress-turned-promotions director Vivian Ventura. Eva was reserved and everything about her was buttoned-up and just so – the little Chanel dress, the jacket, the neat gloves and the small but stylish bag. It was all a little too perfect for my taste. After a while it was all too annoying and I just couldn't keep quiet any longer. 'Hey sister, why don't you undo your jacket and breathe a little?' I told her rudely. 'Let out that wild animal inside you!' That refined prissiness had just got to me.

She looked at me and in elegant English tinged by a careful East European accent she said, 'You know what, darling? That's exactly what I am going to do.' At last! She actually spoke – and what was more, she agreed with me. It was just hilarious and I was delighted, and from that moment on we were the best of friends. Like a Hungarian

Marlene Dietrich, she would always call me 'darling'. She became one of the few people in the world who got to know all my secrets. Some of them haven't even made it into this book – and she's the only person who knows which ones I've kept to myself.

The French film-maker Patrice Leconte once said that true friendship is not something that you can express in words – it's to be demonstrated. And that's how it was with Eva. I'm tall and blonde, she's small and dark but we feel as if we're twins. To look at us you'd think we have nothing in common but we've often laughed until we cried about things we share. Ours was a friendship which opened up another new world for me, one I'd only seen on television shows like *Dallas*. She was a countess from an old Hungarian family who used to own vast tracts of Transylvania until a hundred years or so ago. They lost everything by the end of World War II, but her family tree was full of barons, princes and counts. She was the real aristocratic deal and when I first met her she had recently married an English lord who lived in London's exclusive Eaton Place. I often preferred to sleep at her place rather than in a hotel when I was in town. She had a couch that was just a two-seater so my long legs would drape over it, but she always made it up with pillows and blankets for me; it was so cosy.

Through her I got to know Prince Michael of Kent, cousin of the Queen, when we both attended the same function. At that time I was completely enraptured by Russian literary giant Alexander Pushkin; I had devoured his biography and, heart beating, had learned of his death as a result of a dual over his wife. I was very sad at the time and I had fallen hopelessly in love with a romantic poet who died more than 150 years earlier. It was completely impossible, but it felt as real as if he were living now. Prince Michael might not have been quite so passionate about Pushkin the man, but he was also a huge fan of his work. For him I guess it was all to do with the influence that Pushkin exerted as one of the last Russians to be accepted in England.

I was invited to private parties where I would meet Ministers of State, key figures in the business world responsible for billions and royalty. American limos looked cheap and over-the-top next to the guests' elegant English Rolls-Royces driven by chauffeurs immaculate down to the tips of their white gloves. And it was thanks to Eva that I got to travel in that world.

I wouldn't have otherwise been permitted inside a very exclusive, private London casino founded in 1828 by William Crockford and the Duke of Wellington. Crockfords is in an unremarkable-looking town house like many others from the Victorian era but when you step inside and on the thick, red carpet you're immediately back in that era at its most opulent. I'd guess that a year's membership would be the equivalent to a good salary for many. Everything is tastefully done, down to the delicious restaurant and the punters were well-dressed, smoking cigars and sipping Cognac. Games included poker and blackjack played on a handful of tables around which even the spectators radiated power and importance. Crockfords' discreet charm was unexpected if you only knew casinos from the plastic emptiness of Las Vegas.

The minimum bets were colossal and Eva and I were content to watch the game of the charming man who had invited us that night, but he wanted the two of us to join in with him on the roulette table and passed us a thick bundle of money. I put my stake on 15 – for my birthday of 15 July – and it came up. They gave me a teetering stack of chips – I mean, it was just insane. I hadn't looked closely at what we'd put down but it was probably something like £1,500. The winnings were quite intimidating and I squealed uncontrollably, flapping about. Then we got to see the real money, and I was thinking *My God! You could buy a house with this!* Once I calmed down my polite Danish upbringing took over and I handed our host the cash.

'Oh please,' he said with an air of finality. 'You won that.' And that was typical of the circle I was moving in. Unlike so many people I'd come across who were rich but in another way so cheap, wealth didn't matter to them. They didn't make me feel the weight of things, there was nothing I had to give in return. So Eva and I, we split the riches between us. Yet I couldn't quite shake off the feeling that something was about to happen. Perhaps I would be made to feel I had to go to bed with him – you know, some kind of subtle demand – but it never happened.

Eva also had connections with the world of horses. We got invited to Ascot, to polo matches and to one of England's biggest stud farms owned by Eva's friend and her husband. It was really over-the-top. My bedroom overlooked the fields where there must have been 400 horses placidly enjoying the day. The house was just as impressive: the guest room I was given was the size of a large hotel suite, situated on the first floor with an uninterrupted view over the beautiful rolling fields. I was flabbergasted but like the rest of Eva's crowd, the owners made me feel completely at home. It was a much-appreciated opportunity to recharge my batteries. What a contrast from my gaudy life in Hollywood and all the lovelier for being so unexpected. Their kindnesses won my heart and I felt protected although I always knew that it wasn't a life in which I could be more than a tourist.

I saw a completely different type of Englishman when I played at a club in Manchester. Simply Red singer Mick Hucknall was out for the night with his friends and we hung out after my set, talking about music and wandering the streets of his Manchester together. It was the opposite of the gentrified country life with all these freaked-out hippies smoking joints and I thought, *this is* so *me*. Wow! I couldn't believe how I was fitting into these different social situations. After my time with the aristocracy, Mick was refreshing. We ended up going back to his place in Manchester and it was very much the laidback musician's pad – all warm colours, joints going around and candles. As soon as he had suggested going back, his friends agreed. They were all really nice – there was no edge to anyone and we just chatted and relaxed.

The night reminded me of a grander version of how I had lived with my first husband Kasper. Very comfortable, very freestyle – nobody was judged on how they looked or who they were. It got to about 3am and people started to drift away while others curled up where they were on sofas to sleep. There was no way I was going to leave for London at that time and Mick said, 'I'm going to have a bath – do you want to join me?'

'I'd love to!' I said, thinking, *This is weird...* but at least it was a variation on being asked to go to bed. He lit up yet more candles in his purple bathroom, cranked up some music, and then we were in the water together. Now Mick Hucknall is many things but one thing he's not is a very good-looking guy, however what he does have is this expression of someone who knows he's totally outrageous and yet very friendly, really cool. So I was just winging it and there we were, taking a bath together. We talked about ourselves and nothing happened. To be honest, even if you'd paid me I couldn't have gone to bed with the guy. He was more than that – we became friends and I did stay in contact and we met up years later – but we did have a great hot bath together. I thought, *I'm really back on track! It's possible just to be with someone and sit in a purple room having a bath and just get to know someone who's brilliant and makes wonderful music.* It was such a good moment, just hugging, talking and music.

This was, in general, a time when my life was unpressured, happy and low-key. I always had Eva by my side. In the spring of 1989, she came to the Cannes International Film Festival. I had been hired by New Line Studios to promote a project inspired, like *Red Sonja*, by Marvel Comics: *She Hulk*. They still needed something like $5 million to get the film off the ground and we were going to raise awareness among investors. As usual, I'd left everything to the last moment. I didn't want to go and alone so I called Eva: 'Countess, will you come to Cannes?'

'But of course, darling,' she said.

'You have to be ready in, like, three hours,' I told her.
Poor girl! She always had to pick out her Chanel finery and
it would take her forever to get her luggage together – I was
always calling her with minutes to spare. One way or
another, she made it and it was great to see her. We kissed
and hugged each other and gossiped about boys and vowed
to kick up a storm at Cannes.

The next morning I had a photocall at 11 o'clock and I
was in She Hulk green make-up. Like Superman, my
character was to have an alter ego: an ordinary girl in
glasses who becomes Hulk when she gets freaked out, which
wasn't so far from what I was feeling for real. Where 20
photographers were expected, it looked like a couple of
hundred had turned up: it was a vintage scene of Cannes
chaos. Someone had the bright idea of putting me on a boat
so that everyone could get a picture from the shore – can
you imagine a more ridiculous sight? So I was floating out
there, waving greenly like an idiot to all those paparazzi
who were jostling for position on the bank and swarming
onto a pier to get a better picture. They were shouting,
climbing over each other and, inevitably, the pier gave way
and collapsed into the water, taking with it the camera gear
of photography's finest. It was beyond absurd and actually
pathetic. *What were they doing all that for?* I thought to
myself, *I'm not worth that. All that waste, all that
equipment – to what end?* I really didn't get a kick out of
being the centre of that kind of attention: I didn't belong at
all. It was a fucking nightmare.

In the end the production company didn't get their $5

million and we never made the movie – that's the bullshit of the movie industry. But at least the Countess and I had a week together. And in the evenings we went to parties which were full of stars, famous producers and eminent directors. We would first go to a restaurant and discuss where we were going to hang out later. You might on any night, as we did, find the next table being taken by Sean Penn and Charles Bronson. It was incredible to see such legends for real, but I only had eyes for Sean. He didn't have classic good looks but there was just something about him. He had the air of someone who was hiding something and I thought, 'He does look hot!' Eva and I giggled together, trying to catch their eyes whenever we could.

Eva started talking with Charles but I wasn't talking so much with Sean and dinner was soon over. They went and the two of us were left feeling rather flat, having hyped ourselves up for something to happen. Maybe we thought we'd got them. 'What are we going to do now?' I asked. 'Shall we head back to the hotel or maybe hit a club?' We decided to go dancing. The night was buzzing, there were cocktail parties everywhere and I had on a tight dress made out of silver threads, stilettos (also silver) and diamond jewellery. My hair was simple and my make-up was beautiful. It was one of those nights when I knew that I looked as good as I felt: I was totally ready to take over Cannes! We picked our club almost at random but when we sat down we looked up to see... Sean Penn and Charles Bronson. It was crazy and in my pushy way somehow I ended up sitting next to them. The Countess disappeared and I'm not really sure what happened with her that night. All I knew was I was alone with Sean that night in the club, sitting at an old wooden table into which he carved messages with a knife. Then it was my turn. I answered whatever it was he'd asked and we had a conversation at that table.

I was completely sold on him – completely. And the point was very clear: am I going to go with the guy or not? It was purely sexual. It was very hot. I would have done anything for him. Then the club was closed and we were in a car. And I thought, *Go for it... Why not? You adore him, you'll probably never see him again, but that's fine. That's Cannes. That's it*. And that's what I did.

We spent an outrageous night together in Sean's hotel room. Without going into details, it was just what I wanted. Awesome. We woke up to someone knocking loudly on the door in the morning. I couldn't see who it was when Sean answered but I certainly heard them yell at him. It was a female voice and afterwards I would sometimes wonder if it had been Madonna, but I really don't know. Sean slammed the door shut, turned and simply asked, 'Would you like breakfast?'

'I would love some breakfast,' I told him. So we ate together and that was it. He was to leave the next day and I knew I would probably never see him again, but it had been such a great time. That was okay. I didn't feel guilty and I knew then that whatever anyone says, women are just as capable as men of having a good time without getting involved. That said, I've not had many one-night stands. Basically, I'm more suited to long-term relationships despite that night with Sean and the way the media paint me as wildly promiscuous.

It was once alleged that I had been offered a million dollars by a man who wanted me to sleep with him – a journalist had seen Robert Redford and Demi Moore in *Indecent Proposal* too many times, I'd say. Though, to be honest, if someone was to give me that much money, I'd probably go for it. Hey – one night, you'd get over it. But there were always those kind of stories. It was even said that I was a prostitute. Years later, when I was married and living in Switzerland, I received a phone call from the Swiss police who told me the Italian authorities needed to talk to me about a criminal case. I was terrified. At the time I was pregnant with Raoulino, my fourth and final child.

My name had come up in a French court case. I hired a lawyer and discovered that a prostitute ring in France had been linked to major film stars and it was alleged that I was one of the girls. It was a bit like a European version of the Heidi Fleiss case in the States. Eventually the French authorities wrote to my representative apologising for having dragged me into it and said it had been a mistake. But what I thought was so unfair was that for some people I would always be linked to that case. It didn't matter how much anyone said that it wasn't true. There will always be people who look at my most highly-charged images and think – that must be Gitte.

CHAPTER 17

THE PERFECT FAMILY

In the spring of 1992 I was asked to do a music show in Milan called *Castro Cardo*. This was quite a step up for me: they only asked people who really knew about music and could handle a major production. I was surprised and delighted to be asked and immediately agreed. *Castro Cardo* was a showcase for the best of the more old-fashioned singers and bands in Italy. It wasn't unlike a very posh forerunner of *X Factor*, but for established acts who were called up by experts from the worlds of opera and classical music. Acts found it hard to get on, not least because it only went out once a year and an appearance meant they were destined for great things.

My co-host was a real pro, able to deal with anything that happened on live television, and the show went really well. The critics were complimentary and I had universally good coverage in the press. Even those writers who had a reputation for shooting down presenters were nice. On the night I was on a real high and when we went off-air, I returned to my dressing room for a much-needed drink of water. The studio was next to a lake and it was really humid. I was exhausted when I opened the door to hear my phone ringing.

'*Ciao*, it's Roberto.' A voice from my career as a model. It was Roberto Lansorti, who had an agency for catwalk models. He was about five foot tall and built like a bulldog, but a really nice guy. I had always got on well with him and felt that he was completely trustworthy but it had been something like 15 years since we'd last talked.

'*Roberto*! How did you get me here?'

'I've got my ways…' he laughed. 'Hey Gitte, amazing show!'

'I know,' I said. I felt it had gone brilliantly.

'There's a bunch of us about to get together, old friends…' It all sounded really nice.

'I would love to,' I said. But I was completely drained and they were all the way over at Lake Como, where the rich and famous of Milan would, as Roberto did, have a holiday home, it wasn't realistic. 'Maybe another time.' And then he started guilt-tripping me.

'Well. You – you're rich, you've just had one of your biggest evenings ever…' – he knew I felt uncomfortable with all the trappings of success – 'rich' is a big word to me. 'You don't have time for me? Why don't you just do what a star does? Pick up your phone, order a helicopter and you'll be here in 30 minutes.' Typical of Roberto. Whatever was going down, if there was an obstacle he would find a way around it. He meant it in a nice way but it really got to me. Though actually, why not? I've never liked to let things get in my way either. *Go on*, I thought, *get out of your fucking dressing gown, get out of the studio and go to your old friends.*

Half an hour later I was in the helicopter. There was a couple of thousand dollars less in my purse but it was pretty exciting: for once, it was all about me. I wasn't getting the ride for someone else, it was me going for myself. It was a good decision – the party at Roberto's was fun, cosy and it was great to see people I hadn't seen for years. Such great memories resurfaced.

There weren't that many people there and the one stranger stood out: a muscular but skinny guy from Switzerland. He was a friend of some influential designer in Milan, which was how he'd been invited. Coincidentally, I found out much later, he'd been flatmates with my first serious boyfriend Luca and his name was Raoul. He was sweet, he was definitely with the programme and he was kind of cute.

Raoul didn't talk about modelling or movies. He reminded me a bit of Eva in that he introduced me to a whole new scene when he started talking about motor racing. I'd seen Formula One on TV, but that was about the extent of my knowledge and it was so refreshing not to talk about my life and what was going on with me. As usual I was soon flirting with him and being Danish, got us to the pool where I stripped down to my underwear and dived in. 'Are you gonna join me?' I called. Pushy – *very* pushy. It was a bit stupid but it was fun. Raoul seemed rather shy and he stayed by the side of the pool while we talked. When the party ended I went to my room and reflected on how unexpectedly pleasant the evening had been.

Roberto was an excellent host and laid on fabulous food for his guests. Brunch was waiting when I got up to find everyone relaxing and just doing their own thing. All the running around, the helicopter ride, the cocktails had got to me and I was feeling tired, but all my energy returned when I saw that Raoul hadn't gone home either. *Let's see what he's up to*, I thought. He spotted me and came over.

'Thank you for last night, that was really good,' he said. 'You look great this morning.' That was the right thing to say and I wondered why he hadn't gone home yet. But whatever might be in store, it was good that he was still there. Perhaps we might even end up leaving Roberto's together. Raoul asked me what I was doing – I had a meeting with a popular Italian jazz and pop singer called Zucchero. After that I was working. Then I just said, 'Why don't you come with me.' I'd arranged for a Mercedes Cabriolet to be sent to the villa for me and I was feeling completely over-the-top. *Why*, I thought, *wouldn't this Raoul want to come with me?*

But he did seem a little hesitant, though it was only because he'd brought along his new Harley-Davidson. 'Can't leave the bike here,' he said apologetically. 'It's not gonna work.'

'Man, come on! Find a way and join me,' I said sharply, jolted out of the moment. I thought his answer ridiculous. 'I'm gonna go get my bags. Here are the keys to the car. When I come back, if you're in the car you're coming with me, if you're not... have a nice life!'

There were many occasions over the next few years when I would come to wish that I hadn't run downstairs with my bags to find the keys in the ignition and Raoul sitting there. But there he was. That was the beginning of something that over the next 14 years of my life would become uncontrollable. Unstoppable. But to begin with it was fun, outrageous and romantic.

After my interview for TV we drove to Lake Garda, where we had time to take a boat ride, just the two of us, before we checked into a villa. A late refuge for Italian dictator Mussolini, it's now one of the most exclusive hotels in the country. Villa Feltrinelli is not far from the shore, situated behind hundred-year-old trees and very pretty: you could see how the position of the place might have appealed to a dictator in trouble. Now it's very chic and superstars appreciate being able to get to it only by boat. Tom Cruise and Katie Holmes stayed there for weeks and other guests have included David and Victoria Beckham.

Despite the protective tree-line, the view from the suite was a stunning sweep of the lake. The history of the place was everywhere. It was packed with books and old pictures lined the walls. If you wanted you could learn all about Hitler's relationship with Mussolini, their successes together and what led to their ultimate failure. And it was in that hotel that Raoul and I spent our first night together: we would go on to spend virtually every day in each other's company for years.

Raoul then lived in a very small apartment in Milan's San Siro district. He shared his place with a girl – he didn't say girlfriend – who was from Iceland and who he seemed to be arguing with. I didn't get involved with his situation but I did continue to see him. Over a week he was good to me but at the end of it I had to go back to LA. That was where I was based and he was in Italy so we both knew the end was coming.

The phone calls started as soon as I returned to LA. It drove me crazy and I thought I'd been stupid to give him not only my number at home but my car phone too. He'd ring off and then ring again immediately – it was utterly infuriating. The whole thing was out of proportion to the few days we'd spent together. He'd introduced me to his sister before he left and when their mother said that she hadn't heard of me he was none too pleased with her. She was just a little old lady and if nothing else, I should have wondered how he was going to behave towards me.

It was the same on the phone. He was very macho and if he was on my mind a lot it was only because I didn't have that much going on after work and I'd be at home thinking about Julian, about how I was going to keep up my place on my own, about my parents and I began to think maybe Raoul wasn't so bad. I was mixed up about how I felt about him but I wanted to think the best. I painted a picture for myself in which everything looked optimistic when it would have been better to take a more objective view but I was still pretty close to never getting back to him. Then he made that one extra call which made the difference. On impulse I snatched the phone up. It changed everything.

'*What?*'

'It was so nice to be with you,' said Raoul. 'I've been thinking about you a lot. You're so far away and you love it so much in Italy – you're a big star. Why don't you come back? You could be safe and comfortable here, your parents would only be a couple of hours away; the kids would be able to see more of you. Think about it.' He was really pushing all the buttons. And I thought, *Yeah, well, he's got a point. It wouldn't hurt to give it a go.* The endless commuting between jobs in the US, Italy and London was draining and it would be good to be closer to friends and family, if nothing else. And with that, a long and increasingly sad chapter of my life started.

It opened with the discovery that the Icelandic girl was still in his apartment. That was a good start. What on earth was he doing inviting me to Milan when he still lived with someone? I checked into a hotel, Raoul came by whenever he could and I continued working between Italy and London. It was always refreshing to get back from a long stint in the UK to catch up together and it kept things between us exciting. He raced a lot and the doubts in my mind soon began to melt away. I was busy and enjoying how different this relationship felt.

He took me for a ride on the Harley-Davidson and from my perch behind him, with the sound of the engine deep and powerful, Milan looked beautiful. I felt so comfortable. 'I want to show you something,' Raoul said. 'I want to take you to where I come from.' That was the day that decided the next 14 years.

He took me over Lake Como and into Switzerland to Lake Lugano. I would get to know it very well but I don't think it ever looked quite so stunning as it did that first day. I was totally overwhelmed by the romance and instead of surfacing to take a reality check, I let myself be carried along in the fantasy. Despite the success of my career what I really wanted was the stability represented by my parents' relationship. I wanted Denmark, or rather the security and comfort I remembered, and it was a longing that I now know I could never fulfil – my childhood was very different and while I'm my parents' daughter, I lived my own life. I could never be like them but I ached for that existence and so I determined that I wouldn't give up on this new relationship whatever happened.

'You know what? We should really have a house by the lake, Gitte.' It sounded wonderful but – aha! – I should have been wise enough to leave some space for myself. I didn't. 'It's so hectic in Milan,' he continued, 'and here you can walk the streets and nobody will know who you are and they won't care anyway. Now isn't that just perfect for you? And it's so close.' That was true – it was barely 45 minutes from the centre of Milan. I gazed out at the tranquil beauty of the lake and well, what was a poor girl to do? I was really torn. Should I settle down? What about my parents, my kids? The lake rippled gently and the sun shone and warmed me down to my toes – it was really too much like a movie. Raoul was so attentive to me – I thought it was amazing that he had taken the time to show me something so important to him and I thought about how Julian could come and stay from Denmark whenever he wanted. Killian would have a safe place to call home. I even started to think about having kids with Raoul – we could have a secure environment here and the schools were good. All those thoughts were running through my mind far too quickly. A balanced, normal life for a family. It would be a great place to rest between shooting movies and to see my parents.

So, yes, we did find a house in the small fishing village of Morcote and shortly after I became pregnant with another boy – Douglas.

CHAPTER 18

BIG DREAMS

Near Morcote was a large villa perfectly situated by the shore of Lugano and it was badly in need of some tender loving care. There were four walls and a roof, but it had been abandoned for years. We would have to renovate the whole thing and getting it perfect would become a real passion. By the time we were ready to move in I was only a few months away from giving birth to Douglas. I was overwhelmed by happiness.

Work on the house had been expensive but now the child who was going to live in it was on his way. This was meant to be. I reaffirmed the solemn promise to myself: no running away this time. No matter what happens, I'm staying with this guy. I was serious – I couldn't keep packing my bags when things got hard; this was something I could give to my kids. This was, by the way, a very big mistake on my part but that was how I was determined to live.

My dream of family life was reality. In my eyes it was taking on the shape of the ideal relationship that my parents enjoyed, only in grander surroundings. It was a good time that made me feel unbelievably happy and I couldn't wait to give Killian and Julian their sibling. I'd got to six and a half months and that was when my waters broke.

It was an afternoon and we were moving the last of our things into the big house. I could never sit still, even when I was pregnant. Ever the busy bee, I was up and down and totally absorbed in what I was doing. Contractions started and I was rushed to the hospital, where my doctor and gynaecologist were standing by. They quickly decided that the only thing for it was to do an emergency caesarean section.

Three months premature, Douglas was tiny and very weak and the medical staff didn't pretend that he had a great chance of survival. The gynaecologist, who together with his wife ended up becoming friends of mine, later told me it was actually better to have a child that early than in the eighth month. Nearer the time of birth an important hormone in the lungs is off doing other work in the brain, I think, and with the bones.

As it was, Douglas's tiny lungs were just fine with the help of all the technological firepower they could bring to bear. His healthy cries were at first cause for celebration but we were cut short when he abruptly fell silent. The staff crowded around and pulled him off me for tests as he turned blue. I didn't understand what was going on. All I knew was that I was lying there without my child or news of him for hours. What the staff didn't even tell me then was that he had been clinically dead for a full two minutes, but it wasn't hard to guess from the face of the doctor who eventually came to see me that the outlook was bleak.

'It's bad,' he told me. 'It's really bad. We don't have the equipment here to stimulate the lungs, heart and brain of an infant under one kilo. We have called the emergency helicopter to take him to a hospital at Bern [the Swiss capital].'

The mountain weather was poor and we waited until 6 o'clock the following morning for the team to arrive. We spent the whole night praying and crying. I was still too weak to move and I had to stay in my bed while my helpless little baby was flown away.

As I recovered over the next 10 days I watched the other new mothers in the ward cradle their healthy babies as I had done with my two previous boys, but there was nothing I could do except wait. I could hardly move anyway – during the birth the doctors had given me an injection in my leg so that I didn't lactate and they had hit a nerve which had left it temporarily paralysed. As time passed slowly I learned Douglas's chances of survival were much greater but any good news always seemed to be accompanied by a fresh blow. I was told there was an increased risk that he would be brain-damaged. His retinas might be detached and it was not uncommon for such premature babies to be blind.

Raoul drove the 280 or so kilometres between my hospital and the capital, where Douglas was being treated alongside babies weighing as little as 500 grams. Three months went by before he was completely off oxygen and only then could they test him for defects. Time stretched into eternity; every day was a waking nightmare. I had to wait two months before I was able to hold him and care for him.

Finally he was big and strong enough to come home,

though he still needed to be an in-patient on a daily basis. At last I felt like I could be a proper mother. I drove him through the gate of our house and then along the long drive that swept down parallel to the lake and to the house. There, I got out of the car, unbuckled his car seat and reached over into the back seat to pick up his blanket and other things to take him inside. Unknown to me a paparazzi was waiting and snapped Douglas in his car seat while I was rooting around in the back of the car.

They splashed the photo all over the Italian media: 'BRIGITTE NIELSEN ABANDONS NEWBORN BABY'. I broke down. I had never taken anyone to court, but this was too much. How could the press do this to my children? The articles were just horrific and were accompanied by photographs that I thought extremely intrusive.

I took on a lawyer and prepared for the typically drawn-out Italian case, but the verdict came down just two months later: I was defeated. Stunned, but not prepared to give up, I got my team to bring the case again, and once more we lost. To me that wasn't justice. One day, I resolved, I would show the press coverage to Douglas in case he ever decided to become a lawyer.

Douglas's birth was a turning point. The dream I had of my new life was now tinged with shadows but it made me all the more determined that nothing would stand in the way of my happiness and my family. I didn't realise that I was beginning to compromise my sense of what I needed for myself in my rigid determination to maintain the relationship with Raoul at all costs. Had I been watching for it, I might have noticed he was gradually becoming less thoughtful and caring than he had been when we first met, but I was so confident I even told my mum that I would be just like her and Dad. I was staying put.

The year after Douglas was born Raoul and I were married in a registry office. It wasn't a big wedding, but my parents, brother and Eva were there on my side and Raoul's family also came. Even then I wasn't entirely sure about us. It was just a certainty that I had to make this thing work out. Not long after that I discovered that I was pregnant once more.

I couldn't bear to go through all that I had with Douglas again. What if this one was also premature? But there was never any doubt that I would have the child. And this time, with Raoulino, everything was perfect. The pregnancy was easy and he arrived just 10 days before the due date, not long after we had been watching the race in which Formula One legend Ayrton Senna was killed. He had become a friend and I admired the work he did for children in his country. I decided it would be fitting to give Raoulino the middle name of Ayrton in his honour.

With two young children and a good lifestyle to support I felt under pressure to get with the programme as soon as possible and not breastfeed Raoulino for long. Raoul had become my business manager, handling contracts and controlling deals, and that was fine with me: I ran around so much that I needed someone to look after me behind the scenes.

I was the main breadwinner in the family. I didn't get much of a chance to celebrate the joy of motherhood but

Raoul's driving career cost a fortune and one of the ways we covered some of the costs was for me to be the face of one or other of his sponsors.

At the end of my working day I played with the kids and took care of them. I helped them to put up the tent in the back garden and then I would go to them at three in the morning because they were scared. Reading them goodnight stories and telling them I loved them kept me sane. My own mother used to draw a heart on me with her finger, very quickly, almost like a caress. It was an 'I love you' for me and I often did that to the boys. Even when I was worn out I would always make time for them. We had a nanny too but I wanted to be fully involved with their upbringing. Being with them never failed to boost my energy levels.

Raoul's passion was for his racing and I supported him in doing whatever he wanted. At home we weren't so much a two-car as a ten-car family and we had amazing vacations. Raoul taught the boys to ski brilliantly – even Killian, who wasn't his own boy and who I felt was never his favourite. I'd never learned to ski and Raoul had the patience to show the children how to do it properly. He was equally good about getting them to play football and took them to see Inter Milan play in their home stadium. Sport was the aspect of their lives he was most interested in. Now all the boys are excellent skiers and of course they got into go-karting; Ayrton Senna's kids had go-karts so we did too.

The boys were very happy but in truth they wouldn't have had any less fun if they'd been on rented skis. It wasn't good to let them have everything and it was part of what began to make me terribly miserable. Raoul and I should have made those quiet moments that two people need to have when they've got a baby between them. I began to believe that things weren't working but if I wasn't going to break my pledge, what could I do?

There was often a lot of ready cash around and Raoul was efficient in getting payment for me. Minutes before I was due to go on one Danish talk show, he warned the producers that if they didn't get the cash out I wasn't going to do the show.

I would suggest that he might consider taking on more work himself. Maybe he could do something in the motor-racing world. I was quite worried about what we would do if something happened to me. He said everything would be all right, but I had this nagging fear about the kids. They were all at private schools in Switzerland; everything felt such a burden so I grabbed whatever job paid the most. But still I didn't want to leave.

Talking about where we were going in our relationship didn't seem to change anything. Things were getting too much to deal with and it is hard to explain what was happening because it wasn't something that took place in a certain number of weeks or months. An insistent voice in my head told me that this was my last chance to make a family and I owed it to my children, my parents and everyone around me not to give up: I had to keep going. I just made up all these reasons for continuing as things were. *Just get through these hard times*, I thought, *and it will all be perfect*. It *was* perfect already, I told myself: I had a beautiful house, I lived in a wonderful country, I had healthy kids – what was there to bitch about? I found my own way of dealing with my unhappiness.

We usually had a glass or two of wine over dinner. Wine relaxed me and I enjoyed drinking. And of course, when we were at openings or dinner parties we always had cocktails. However, over those years my intake of alcohol increased in proportion to the pressure of work and the guilt I felt about how I was acting as a mother. I could justify my drinking in terms of the accepted culture in our corner of Europe, but then it's hard to say at exactly what point you become an alcoholic: you might not even realise you have a problem for years. Over time one glass of wine became two or three; one cocktail became two. It was a gradual process. And alcohol worked for me: I was angry, furious that Raoul and I were even in the same house. A doctor might have suggested better medication for my frustration but this was my way out.

I've since heard from other alcoholics and people who have lived with them that it's not uncommon to take years to graduate from a glass of wine at dinner to a bottle. So if you have a teenager who drinks a couple of bottles on a weekend with their friends, be careful: that's not okay, watch for those red flags at an early age. I was unusual in developing alcoholism in my mid-30s. Up until then I'd been pretty healthy and watched what I consumed: food as well as drink. But you never know when the devil is waiting around the corner to get you. I told myself that an alcoholic is someone who wakes up with the shakes that don't go away until they've had their first drink of the day and they don't stop swigging until they pass out in the evening. That wasn't me.

I could go anything from a week to a month without a drink but when I did, I would make up for lost time. When I started rehab many years later I learned that it's binging which is really dangerous. The classic alcoholic might be someone who drinks every single day but for a new generation binge-drinking is where it's at. In Europe alcoholism is still taboo. Everybody drinks, but few would say they are alcoholic.

I evolved my own system of drinking. On some occasions it would even be as long as two months before I got together with a friend and we might, for example, enjoy a post-work glass of wine and we would finish with a bottle. Then another bottle. And then I would feel sick and not have anything for the next few weeks.

At work I was totally professional. I never drank – I wouldn't have been able to remember my lines if I had, there was no question about it, but the minute I was out of that studio door, I was ready to boogie. For me, as with many alcoholics, there was always something to celebrate or to commemorate. Toasting special occasions is perfectly acceptable and that's what makes it so deadly for the alcoholic looking for an excuse. I was becoming so sad, and the monkey on my back was the booze: It had the answer to all my worries. It was always there to make me feel better as the relationship with Raoul fractured. I might have gone that way later or perhaps it might never have happened, but I was giving up.

There's something particularly degrading about a woman – a mother – who finds herself lying on the sofa in the middle of the afternoon. She's not drunk as such, but she's getting there and she doesn't feel like doing anything. I'd always been that busy bee, full of energy, unstoppable. I don't know how I did it to myself. Saying I had become a couch potato would be making light of it – I was a slave to my own misery.

I didn't have the energy to do anything and that made me feel even worse. I was weak and I was embarrassed by my lack of motivation. The sort of tiredness that overwhelmed me defies description. It almost made me frightened, as if I might put so much effort into standing up that I would drop dead.

When I wasn't working I increasingly confined myself to the house. That meant not doing anything for the boys that didn't involve meals for them, putting them to bed or doing puzzles with them. Raoul or the nanny had to deal with everything else. Ironically, I probably did need some time to myself but the way I was carrying on was doing me no good at all.

By the time the marriage had virtually broken down I had resorted to hiding the extent of my drinking. I concealed bottles around the villa but then I would forget where the stash was. As an alcoholic you become so primitive – it's all so obvious and it was disgusting. I wonder now how it was possible for me as a mother to become such a ridiculous figure. Raoul knew what was happening and was furious.

I would deny it all. 'No, no, I don't drink,' I'd say in a little voice, after he'd seen me hastily move a bottle out of sight. It was unbearable that he could now take the moral high ground over me. If I was already drunk when he started having a go at me I would become a different person and swear at him. I was not a nice person to live with, but he certainly didn't reach out.

I was nothing more than a burden to him and to the children as well. *I was a fool*, I thought, *a joke to everybody. It would be better if I wasn't there.* On one occasion we had an argument and I lost my balance and fell down the stone stairs to the kitchen. I lay in front of the kids thinking that I'd really hurt myself. It wasn't good news. The following day I was due to begin a chat show in Denmark – *Gitte and Friends* (*Gittes Venner*, as it was known in Denmark). The idea was I would have a relaxed, two-hour chat with a guest and I needed to be totally fit but I could feel that I'd banged my foot up. It wasn't broken, but it had a wound that went down to the bone.

When Raoul left to go racing, I wrapped up the damage as best I could and thank God, was able to escape to Denmark for a while. A friend spotted something wrong when I got to the studio and I tried to hide it, worried about what the production team might think.

'Come on!' he said. 'Show me the foot.' I waited until we'd wrapped for the day and he and I drove to my parents' place. We got the shoe and dressing off to see pus oozing out of the battered foot. It was a mess, but I insisted that I was fine.

'You cannot go on with the series like that,' he said. 'Things may not be okay, but you have to deal with the situation.' He was right. I was extremely proud of the show I'd got and was looking forward to showing Copenhagen to the famous friends and contacts I'd built up who were to include Joan Collins, John Cleese, David Hasselhoff, Jeremy

Irons and Catherine Deneuve. We were to shoot in Hotel d'Angleterre, where I'd once been with Sylvester. I was in Denmark with a great programme ready to go and there I was, I thought, turning alcoholic with one mangled foot and a fucked-up marriage. I hid behind huge sunglasses turning over all the options in my mind.

I told the Nordisk Films producers that I'd fallen over while out running about with the kids. They got a private doctor who cleaned up my foot, gave me painkilling injections and a couple of stitches and said I'd be okay. And I was. The foot throbbed as it healed but I even felt a sort of cleansing, as if there was pus deeper inside me which had been wiped away. The production team and I enjoyed a lovely dinner and finally, I felt ready to rock. I ended up back at my hotel with my friend and the mini-bar. There, I polished off all the little bottles and he had a glass of champagne. I was still drinking but it was the first time in a long while that it was accompanied by positive thoughts.

We had a safe in the house where we kept all the income from the cash jobs. Raoul didn't want me to get money for alcohol so he changed the combination on that. I was reduced to tears by the safe, uselessly spinning the wheel to guess the new code, but then I guessed it and my first thought was *That's it! I'm taking the money and I'm going back home to Denmark to live with my parents*. I opened the door and stopped, looking at the pile of money. Who was I fooling? This was my money, this was my house: I wasn't stealing from him, I was stealing from myself. And I realised that my drinking was stealing everything from myself – my zest for life, my sense of humour, my intelligence, my straightforwardness. I was losing everything. I would take what was mine and go home and the kids would have to live with the nanny.

I was overwhelmed with the alcoholic's miserable sense of guilt and embarrassment at my behaviour. I had to sneak into my own safe to get money to buy a ticket to see my mum. How low had I sunk? I was devastated. I didn't go back to Denmark, of course. The drinking just got worse and I became more afraid of the world. I couldn't speak on the phone and I needed a drink before I was able to face anyone. My self-esteem was zero and I was constantly in tears. The simplest things terrified me – even saying 'Hello' to a friend on the street made me think I was going to end up looking stupid in some way.

The worst times of all were those occasions – fortunately not many – when I would call my mum to hear her patiently interrupt my stories with, 'Darling... Gitte... this is the fourth time you've called today and you're telling me exactly the same story.'

Out of everything, I'm most ashamed that I stopped going to parent meetings at school: I didn't show up for student shows or their sports days and I never went to social events. I felt like I might as well lie down and die – I had no connection with anyone. I'd given up on life, on myself, on everything, and I had been such an outgoing person.

I carried on working but when Raoulino was diagnosed with a brain tumour I wasn't there for him. I betrayed him for the bottle. Today, I look back at that time as being a big, black hole. I wasn't there in those months when Raoulino was in hospital and the doctors tried desperately to save him. Yet I loved him more than anything, as paradoxical as that sounds. I had drowned my personality and my sense of self-preservation.

After undergoing numerous therapies and following different methods for overcoming the sense of shame and guilt over the years, I have had to face up to those three months when I was absent as a mother. It was impossibly difficult to do but that was a crucial part of my eventual recovery. I had to go through all that to win back the love and respect of Raoulino and a day did come when he was able to say, 'Mum, come on! You didn't drink that much.'

'Yes, I did,' I said.

'You know what? Maybe you did,' he told me, 'but you were always there for me anyway.'

It would take us a long time to reach that point when he could forgive me, but from then on, our relationship would be stronger than ever.

It's one of the toughest things you do as a recovering alcoholic, learning to live with the things you can't change. There were so many things that I would have loved to have done differently in those years. Most of all, I should have left Raoul, but I'd got to the point where I didn't care about life itself any more.

CHAPTER 19

'THE SHOW MUST GO ON'

In 1998 I was hired to do some big variety television shows in Spain, where I was more known as a singer than an actress. I've always found the country to be really relaxed and I've had so many great times there. I was excited to have a reason to go back and particularly looked forward to being able to spend three days in Madrid. My luggage was packed ahead of time and I was ready to give all I had to the shows and to renew the friendships I had over there.

My companion was my bodyguard, Rodolfo. He had been my faithful shadow for years and had become a friend to our whole family. Killian and he had become best friends and it was Rodolfo who taught him kickboxing and other martial arts. We were joined in Madrid by the two other bodyguards, who took us to our hotel. I collapsed into a chair in my room and had a glass of the champagne that was provided for me whenever I visited. It was such a relief to be welcomed and to be looking forward to a job.

I started going over the songs in my head and began humming to myself. It was the start of a long haul. The Spanish have this crazy tradition of shows that run from 8pm and only finish in the early hours – and they were live. I went on at 9pm, came back halfway through and finished up around 1.30am. I was tired but really happy and when I was done saying goodbyes, I only wanted to head straight back to the hotel. There, I ran a bath and washed off all the sweat but my mouth still ached from the formal kisses – it was three kisses goodbye, the Spanish and Italian way. When I was done Rodolfo was still on duty.

'Well done!' he said. 'Great show.' I called home the next morning to find out how the kids were doing. They were fine but Raoul wasn't around, which was great as I didn't really want to go through him to get to talk to the boys.

I worked my ass off for the rest of the day and the show followed that evening. Afterwards, I called Raoul and we agreed to meet in Rome for the next big show. There was no affection between us at all by then, but when I arrived he looked even less happy to see me than usual.

We got to the car and he leaned over the bonnet. 'I've got something to tell you,' he said. I could see in his eyes that something was badly wrong as he looked away and down. 'Your dad is dead.'

'Whaddya mean?' I muttered nonsense, thinking that whatever he had to tell me couldn't possibly be what he seemed to have said. Everything started to move quickly. I yelled and screamed in reaction to the shock. Somehow, I found myself in the passenger seat of the car, then I was weeping and perhaps I felt I could somehow shake the news out of my head, but I was banging my head again and again on the dashboard. I knew it was true.

The man had been my rock: he had supported me and guided me through every decision I'd ever made about my life; played badminton with me as a child and always counted the number of times we could volley the shuttlecock over the net – the record was 143, I remembered that. The strictness of his rules was more than matched by the deep and profound love he had for his children.

It had freaked me out when I was young and he told me, 'Gitte, you don't need to worry about anything.' We had never discussed my unhappiness about school but I'm sure that's what he meant. 'You're not from here.'

'What do you mean, Dad?' I asked. He surprised me so much my eyes were wide.

'You're from far away, from up in the skies, from a different planet.' Now this was bizarre. 'You're completely your own, you're very special, *Gitte-mus*,' he said, the Danish for 'little Gitte-mouse'. With that he gave me a big hug. He knew in some way that I was not like everyone else and he wanted me to celebrate that. I never forgot his imaginative and encouraging vision. He worked tirelessly to provide everything for his family.

Saturdays as a child had meant that me and my brother would go to the store where I could indulge my love for liquorice. Dad liked his sugar-free peppermint gum and would buy a brand of salty liquorice called Piratos which he left on the table, open, telling us that they were his and we couldn't have them. He knew, of course, that my brother and I would never resist taking some while trying to make it look as if the packet was undisturbed, but that was okay, he only meant to tease us.

And my mother... my God, they had been together 36 years! The thought pulled me back into myself and the car. Mum had tried to get hold of me in Spain without success and had called Raoul. She told him it was urgent and that she had to get hold of me immediately. I felt myself becoming hysterical. If we hadn't have been driving already I'd have got out of the car at once. I couldn't breathe properly. Again I banged my head repeatedly on the dashboard. There was no way I would be able to do the show. 'I want to go to Denmark now!' I was screaming again but the contract with the television company was watertight.

The producers had told us that the show, as they say, must go on. They had to fix my make-up. My tears had smudged my mascara and my eyes were red and puffy. I remember nothing about the show itself apart from it finishing about half past midnight but I'll never forget the aching sense of loss. We still had to get back.

It was 650 kilometres from Rome to Lugano and I had done the journey countless times. I knew it meant going 18 hours without much in the way of rest. Now that familiar trip and the passing hours became unbearable. I spent the entire ride on the phone to my mother, crying and talking, talking and crying.

Back at the villa, despite my lack of sleep I paced around worrying about how I was going to tell the boys that their grandfather was dead. I had to get some rest and lay down on the sofa in the living room but I couldn't shut my mind off. There was another programme to do that night, a dance show, and I had a contract for 16 episodes. I'd be interviewing the dancers between numbers, but it had to be light and funny. The contract with this one meant that it too couldn't be cancelled so I was to record my part and then fly straight on to Denmark the following morning to be at my mother's side for the funeral.

After the service at the church my father was laid to rest in a beautiful part of the grounds. I wandered around aimlessly, trying to remember the names of those family members I hadn't seen in years. My brother Jan looked like he had been crying as much as I had and my brave, strong mother looked unbelievable. Dad had been her first boyfriend – she was 16, he was 18. Now she was organising the food for everyone back at the house they had shared. I held onto her and cried. I didn't want to tell her that I couldn't stay, that I had to fly back first thing the next morning for yet another show.

I flew back with an unfamiliar feeling beginning to lodge itself in my heart. It was hatred: I hated my life. I hated myself even more for not being able to break out of my situation and my addiction to alcohol. Even with my father's death I wasn't able to get up and walk away.

I began to see things very clearly. I knew there was something terribly wrong and I knew that I was too weak to do anything about it. When I looked at myself in the mirror I was overwhelmed by a sense of helplessness. I was totally paralysed, nobody could help me. I began to feel that there might only be one way out. I imagined what it would be like to be at peace, no longer to have to endure the pain of daily life. These thoughts came to me with increasing regularity – and after a while they would be there even when I wasn't drinking.

I'd always dismissed people who turn to suicide as weak and selfish. It was the ultimate act of betrayal and I was very scared. My doctor suggested I get specialist help for the alcoholism and gave me a number of a good psychiatrist. I knew that what the doctor had advised made perfect sense, but when I got home I soon started drinking again and the contact details went in the bin unused.

The doctor meant well and it was my fault for not listening to him, but it was also true that the European medical establishment didn't treat alcohol abuse with the same seriousness as they did in the US. You wouldn't find people so ready to leap up and declare their alcoholism in Switzerland or Italy as their American counterparts. The problem wasn't tackled with the same urgency.

One morning I'd had enough. It was a lousy decision to make, I know, though I could also point at the alcoholism and say it was a sickness and a form of depression. I wasn't thinking straight – even when I wasn't drinking, I was still out of my mind. It would have been an awful thing to do even if I hadn't had kids but when you're in that place then it all makes sense. Suicide is the most selfish and disgusting thing one can do but I was going to try it. And it's important that I say it now, as much as it hurts me, because it's the truth.

CHAPTER 20

A NEW DAY

I was in the bathroom upstairs at Morcote, gazing at myself in the mirror. Lonely and filled with pain, I looked as unhappy as I felt. I wanted to look away from that miserable face, but I didn't. The kids were not at home and Raoul was working on his cars. Little was left of the bottle of Jack Daniel's on the bathroom table. The sounds from the outside world were distant.

I had taken a bottle from the bathroom cabinet. It had been about half-full with the pills that rattled into the glass. I looked out of the window over the lake and thought *That's it. Life is over*. I hated how things had been going over the last six or seven years. The dream house was now a prison; big, empty and full of bad karma, but I had stayed here. I forced myself to like it, the monument to my mission in life of making my marriage work. After things had gone to pieces with Kasper, Sylvester and Mark, this was going to be my family forever – I tried everything to make it work.

I thought about how the kids went to school in Lugano. The town had the cutest little airport from where I often flew for work. We lived in Morcote, an idyllic village of just 200 residents, and my vision was of building my own kind of castle there to keep my children safe. I didn't want them to be exposed to the sort of scrutiny I faced in the press. Whenever we went on vacation the photographers followed us and the little ones found it very upsetting; they were always begging me to make it stop and I wanted them to live undisturbed at home. I liked being hidden away: I could walk around the garden completely naked if I wanted, we could take the kids and dogs into Morcote where nobody bothered us. It would have been the perfect family life.

The figure in the bathroom mirror already looked like one of the walking dead. Guilt had nagged away at me for not being able to maintain that perfect family; I had been trapped. I took the glass and swallowed all the pain-killing pills one by one, then I glanced in the mirror: that weak, defeated alcoholic. I felt so sorry for myself – that's being an alcoholic for you. We all have endless reserves of self-pity, we really do. You can't see it when you're in the middle of it but alcoholics really are the worst people, such bad news; I knew that this person wasn't really me but I didn't have the strength to change things.

I hadn't planned that this would be the day. The urge came over me very quickly and I was dressed as usual in the loose-fitting tracksuit I wore around the house. I had probably just gone to the bathroom and decided there and then to do it: there had been no preparation for this moment. At home I never wore make-up or shoes in contrast to the tight-fitting dresses and stilettos I was known for in public – my work uniform.

Birds lived in huge numbers around the shores of the lake and I could hear the flutter of wings, probably coming from the eaves of a nearby house. I was almost at the end now. *Do everyone a big favour*, I thought, *and disappear. Don't be a burden to the children, your mother or your girlfriends.* Deep within the alcoholic haze I knew I had made the right decision: this was what I wanted and for the first time in a long while, I thought, I had done a good thing. I thought of Marilyn Monroe – she did the same thing and she died, and that was okay.

I hadn't written a suicide note, though I knew I didn't want to have people singing at the service. If I was cremated, should the ashes be scattered over the lake here or taken back to my childhood home in Rødovre? I just didn't care. There was an evil character inside me, whispering that none of it mattered: *You're a bad person. Nobody likes you, you're not doing anything useful on this planet so you might as well get on with it! And you don't have the strength to fight, so just check out.* The voice was speaking the truth. The only thing that was wrong was the way I had been living and what I'd done to my family. Was it really harder to get a divorce, check into rehab and, as they say, get my act together? Yes. Much better to throw myself in the lake – or it would have been if I didn't shiver at the thought of the cold water. Pills and alcohol were best because I'd just get comfortable and go to sleep.

I closed my eyes briefly and saw my children: they deserved so much better than anything I had to offer them.

Quietly, I said my goodbyes to them. The bedroom was nearby and it had a panoramic view of the lake; the radio was on in there and I could hear Celine Dion singing 'A New Day Has Come'. Her crystalline voice floated from the speakers and found its way to the bathroom, but it seemed to be coming at me from much further away. She sang of the greatest happiness in the world. But there would be no new day for me. This was to be my last morning on the planet.

My consciousness was just about hanging on and I felt increasingly relaxed. I could still taste the many cigarettes, the sweetness of the Jack Daniel's, but I couldn't remember what day it was although I thought the kids were in school. There was a slight sense of disappointment that things weren't going a bit faster, but at last I wasn't feeling any pain in my body, just a little flutter in my stomach. Now I was numb – no more worries, no more guilt, no more lies. The world lurched and my legs went from under me. I saw the woman in the mirror disappear and I smiled as I went: I was happy. And I was thinking of Marilyn again – maybe this was what she felt too.

CHAPTER 21
SLOW AWAKENINGS

It was like coming out of the other side of a black hole. Soundless. I couldn't see more than vague shapes and there were no smells. I was spinning around and around. Pain. A phantom pain, just as if I was beginning to feel again. And then sound. What was happening? Something was happening. The prison of darkness was smashed by a painful brightness, razor blades of light. This had to be death and I felt happy.

But why then was I hearing voices? I couldn't understand what they were saying but I started to realise that the light wasn't a celestial glow from God but a welcome back to the misery of earthly existence. My Lugano doctor was shining a light into my eyes and asking me something about how I felt. I answered with quiet little 'yes' and 'no's. Abruptly he brought his mouth close to my ear and his breath was the first thing I really felt since regaining consciousness, its warmth and then his tone when he spoke, reassuring and friendly.

'Was that a suicide attempt?' he asked me softly.

Good question. Anyone attempting suicide in Switzerland had to be logged by law and spend time in a psychiatric hospital. All I cared about at that moment was where the boys were and whether it could really be true that I hadn't managed to get rid of Raoul. Crying, foggy, I had a few words with the doctor and I remember signing some paperwork.

I lay my head back on the pillow, closed my eyes and thought how good it would be not to have to open them again. My doctor went on to report that I'd taken an accidental overdose, but as the darkness closed over me again I thought how both in intent and in fact I had made a very deliberate attempt to die. But here I was again and nothing had changed: my nightmare wasn't over.

The first few days after I woke up in hospital were incredibly exhausting, both physically and mentally. I had to reconcile myself to the choice I'd made to end my problems in the way I had. I hadn't been able to get to grips with life and I wanted it all to go away, but I came to understand that I didn't want to die after all and that I was desperate to make a change in myself, I just didn't know what.

It was about a month later that I began to feel the first glimmer of inspiration. The distance between my inner picture of myself and the real Gitte was vast; that knowledge gave me the strength to try to find myself again.

These days I do regular reality checks to ensure I make healthy choices. It sounds banal, I'm sure, but in the past I didn't think about myself enough – it was all about my husband, schools, money, friends and agents. Of course, I still think about all the different aspects of my life, but now I'm always careful to include myself in the reckoning. I'm also much better about keeping in contact with my girlfriends – I always make time to check in with them and see how they're doing. I've realised you can't do anything for anyone else if you can't look after yourself – that was the bottom line and it's true for all of us.

But when my wonderful doctor left me alone for the first time in the hospital bed and I stared up at the ceiling, I still thought that suicide was the way out. Thank God I was too tired to do anything about it then. I had no idea of what lay ahead for me and if someone had told me that day was the beginning of a new, happy life, I would have laughed at them.

CHAPTER 22

THE ESCAPE

In the immediate aftermath of my release from hospital, I remained depressed, lonely and unhappy. I still couldn't end my relationship with Raoul and we never spoke about what had happened. Meanwhile, I continued to drink to numb myself against reality and soon I was working as hard as ever.

Raoul was to race the Paris to Dakar Rally, which began on New Year's Eve. My assignments included television appearances, speeches, interviews, club openings – once again, whatever I could. Miserable as I felt, I still put on a great Christmas for the children, though.

It's a Danish tradition to cut out Christmas hearts, bake cookies and hand-make nougat and marzipan confections: I used to do that with my own grandparents, decorating the tree and listening to seasonal music. We would put the sweets we'd made into the hearts and hang them on the tree. And Raoulino got very excited when we did that together, pointing out his hearts and telling everyone, 'I made that!' I had a special present ready for whoever of the boys made the prettiest heart – they loved the thought of an extra gift before the big day.

That year was a particularly good one because the rally lasted a month so I knew I had time on my own in my house. I still remember the bubbling feeling of euphoria when I left Raoul in Marseille, France, where he was due to meet the other drivers. He was happy too. I turned my car around, hit the accelerator and sped back to Switzerland. Now I had my space, my children and all that time for myself; it was like being reborn – all the pressure was off. It was while Raoul was away that I got a phone call out of the blue: it was another one of those unexpected opportunities which was to change the course of my life.

The caller was a producer from a major Italian TV station called RAI2, who wanted me to take part in Italy's version of a reality show, *The Mole*. Contestants won money through completing physical challenges while working out which one of them had been planted as a spy to sabotage their efforts. I hadn't heard of reality TV back then and wouldn't have cared less if I had – all I knew was it was to start just as the Paris to Dakar ended and that meant I would be away from Raoul even longer.

The show was straightforward. Contestants didn't know each other beforehand and would share their lives for a minimum of 60 days in a Mexican location. Half an hour of footage would be shown daily on RAI2, supplemented by four hours of live coverage in a primetime slot on Sundays. It was a big production for the station and it was a big opportunity for me, which would open my career out in a whole new direction. My instincts told me this was going to be good, though it would be sad to be apart from the boys for so long. I said 'Yes' there and then, without discussing money or contracts – I was elated to be offered a job that lasted that long.

My gut feeling would prove to be right. This would not only give me the boost I needed to bring my marriage to an end but in the longer term it was through reality TV that I got to work through my demons and the alcoholism that was destroying me. Many people rubbish reality TV, but I can honestly say it saved my life. I don't think there's anyone else on this planet who can say they went through such a profound physical and psychological transformation as I did in front of the cameras. The show would be the tool to pull myself out of the quicksand into which I'd been sinking for so long. I went on to live my life in front of the cameras and I can't think of another woman who was such a candid witness to her many adventures and mistakes. It was healthy, it motivated me and it all started from that one telephone call. My one question was 'Can we smoke?' They told me I could.

The other contestants included names familiar to Italian viewers like Paola Perego, Guido Bagatta and Amanda Lear. And they were a very friendly bunch of famous presenters. On arrival at the set the production crew did, as it turned out, take away our cigarettes as well as our mobiles and passports and of course there was no alcohol allowed. At first I freaked out at the thought of such severity but I got to the final week, which meant I stayed 72 days out there – and I had the best time ever.

I got to speak to the kids every Sunday live on TV and they got to see Mum on the show every day – it was a fun programme with none of the nastiness that characterises some of those formats. I felt so good not drinking; everything seemed better – even the palm trees started to look more colourful after a while. We weren't allowed a TV and there weren't any newspapers. I also spent a few days in solitary in the camp prison when I had plenty of time to think and gather the strength to ask myself what I'd been doing to myself for so long.

My jail hut had a hole instead of a proper toilet and food was restricted to an apple and a bag of rice a day. I slept in a special sleeping bag to protect me from snakes and used the cold shower outside. A small camera crew came to interview me first thing in the morning and to film me last thing at night – when I wasn't allowed to talk – and that was all I had to look forward to for a week. When the sun went down I was left in the dark with the sound of animals all around me and would memorise things to keep me busy, but I'd been through so much shit over the past few years that this basic level of life was almost a relief.

Under my wood floor was a nest of rats and when they realised I was friendly, they started coming up so I left rice out for them. One of them gave birth to a litter right there on the floor. When the camera crew asked me how I was dealing with things I told them I was talking to my friends.

'What friends?'

'The rats!' I was really at ease with what was happening.

I won almost all the challenges I was set and I began to feel pride in myself, particularly because the work was very physical. About a week before we went to Mexico we trained in rock climbing and learned to abseil from a dam – tough for someone like me who doesn't enjoy heights. There was also a mental aspect to the challenge in which they asked for three volunteers and said that we shouldn't go for it if we were claustrophobic, but I always said, 'Yes,' to anything and I really meant it: I wanted to challenge myself. We were all buried and I lasted about 45 minutes down there, breathing through a small hole with dirt around me and the thought of tarantulas and snakes in the immediate vicinity; it was a buzz. Something inside me had woken up.

Even sleeping was a challenge. We were assigned a patch of farmhouse floor under a thin blanket and shared our camp with massive winged insects. The Mexicans said they were *cucarachas*, like the song, which I knew as cockroaches and they were very lively in the mornings. I heard them coming before I saw them with their big legs stamping on the ground like marching soldiers. All I could do was convince myself that all the animals would be my friends and these guys were among them. I was nearest the door and the first thing I'd see when I woke up was a pair of their beady eyes greeting me.

Apart from the cameraman and a doctor – and we weren't ordinarily allowed communication with them – we had no contact with the outside world most of the time. I guess I came over as a nice person because when it got towards the end the producer let me know that the viewers had voted for me to be in the final: 'Is there anything that you'd like to say to your husband and family?'

The decision, which I kept to myself beforehand, was to

say, on television, that it was all over. I'd thought about it all the time in that last week and I knew that if I got on the plane and went back to things as they were, I would be back in the same old rut. I had been sober for three months and I'd really started to live again, but that feeling on its own couldn't sustain me.

So that's how it was that I told Raoul via a live two-way link-up, which was being watched by an audience at home. 'Raoul, I'm so, so sorry that I have to tell you like this…' I was as gentle about it as I could be. He didn't even look upset, but went bright red as if he was embarrassed. I'm sure I'd have been in floods of tears if it had have been me.

The crew were stunned and it made big news in Italy where Raoul and I were seen as the model of a stable family. Now there really was no way back. The press tore into me, reporting that I wasn't behaving like a fit mother. I couldn't explain just why it was the only way I'd been able to break the news.

In the plane on the way back it seemed to me like Gitte, the strong, sensible, capable girl, was returning to me. It was wonderful to feel that I at last had the energy to follow up what I decided to do. My resolve didn't weaken even when I stood face-to-face with Raoul. He was furious and insisted we should try to work things out, but my mind was made up.

I left Morcote with suitcases, clothes, my jewellery and a car, as had become something of a pattern in my life. There was nothing I wanted to be reminded of apart from my children. It was so over. I was always like that – when it's over, it's over and I was ready to move on. Why would I want to waste my time? I had enough to occupy me as it was. There was so much about my life that I wanted to change. I felt compelled to act to make a difference even though I was completely miserable. It was like when I was at school and, despite all the bullying, I would study hard to get good grades. Sometimes that even made the other kids bully me less. Now, though, I had a feeling that I hadn't had in years – that I was going to make it. It was like meeting a dear old friend for the first time in ages.

I left Mexico on 2 April and was back in Milan by the 3rd. I left Morcote the next day and on 12 April I met Mattia – the man I went on to marry.

I had moved into a hotel and whenever I was in bed I would be staring up at the ceiling and thinking about the last 14 years of my life. How could it have gone so wrong? I had let people down so badly; I was so far away from where I wanted to be. I discussed my mistakes at length with my girlfriends. It was very hard, but this was an important cleansing process for me.

One of those friends said, 'Gitte, you have got to move on. It's about time you started to look forward rather than staying stuck in the past. Stop worrying away at it.' She was right. Now I focused on the future. I'd wasted so much energy throughout my life in accumulating possessions that didn't make me happy and weren't of any use. I always got more stuff and to what end? I guess people expected it of me. You had to act in a certain way if you were going to be Brigitte Nielsen and I became trapped in the vicious circle. I needed not to concern myself with what other people thought about me. Now I could be myself – and I loved it.

Being determined to be realistic and positive made me feel lighter, almost as if I had physically lost weight. All of us have a tendency to overcomplicate things: we spend way too much time and energy on the unimportant stuff and we carry it all around with us for too long. We should be making decisions based on how we feel rather than picking away at old wounds. It was an incredible relief for me to consign all that baggage to the garbage bin of history. Within eight days of leaving Morcote I was already looking forward, though it took a little while for me to realise what was happening.

I took the kids to a local restaurant for lunch near Morcote. I knew the owner Mario and had often stopped by. I'm a creature of habit when it comes to eating out and love places which are familiar and safe; and I knew it was family-orientated and the kids enjoyed it as much as I did. There is a tradition of enjoying meals in Latin countries which is perfectly suited to me – everyone is smiley, chatty and likes to know each other's business.

That day Mario was pestering me to meet a friend of his he thought I would really like. He thought this guy would make me feel good and make me laugh but I wasn't having any of it. 'Listen, Mario, I'm going through a miserable divorce and I only just have enough in me to put my life back together. I'm not in the mood to go on a date or even meet any of your friends.'

'It'll be good for you!'

'No, Mario, I'm tired of men.'

I knew it would be good for me to spend some time on my own and with my children and my dogs – they were the only things I cared about now.

'Yeah, well done,' said Mario, 'but you're going to meet him anyway. He's here today.' And he pointed out a man who was approaching our table. Damn! Mario just didn't get it that there was nothing in this world that would make me go on a date right then. Even if the man in question did have dark, warm eyes, a suntan, good skin and an attractive haircut... and not even if he was intelligent, a good conversationalist and funny... Then again... I might be going through a divorce, but it wasn't as if I was dead, was it? But the decider was his age: he was 25.

'My God, Mario!' I said. 'Please, I could be his mother! My oldest boy is 20 – it'll never happen.' But it did – and thank goodness. We ended up having a good lunch and an enjoyable afternoon. I still found it hard to get my head around the age gap, but we swapped numbers.

Afterwards, though, I wondered why young Mattia was interested in me. Was it because I was a celebrity? I'd long been paranoid about people liking me because of my status. And I was 15 years older than him with a couple of ex-husbands in my past and the children and the divorce, all that stuff. Why would anyone want to get involved with that messy set-up? Plus I hadn't exactly been at my best that day: I have a really bad allergy that affects my eyes and they were all runny and red. I wasn't wearing make-up and my hair looked as if I'd been dragged through a hedge backwards. I wasn't supposed to meet anyone!

Mattia called the next day to arrange a date, but I turned

him down and on the next couple of occasions he asked. Even when I did finally agree and he came over to call for me I didn't have the courage to answer the door. I should have just admitted that I'd changed my mind. He was quite rightly really pissed off with the way I was acting. I didn't feel attractive or sexy and I was just not feeling quite on top of things. Not to mention that age gap which still preyed on my mind. No, I couldn't do it.

Our mutual friend Mario called to say, 'He's had enough now. If you want any chance of meeting him, you need to apologise. Meet with him.' I had to admit to myself that I was behaving in an immature way and I wasn't usually someone who played games like that. I relented and Mattia and I went for a drive over the other side of Lugano to Campione d'Italia, a delightful little independent region known for having its own casino and no taxes.

Mattia booked us into a cosy, comfortable Italian restaurant. We had real Italian pizza, with candlelight and music in the background, while we discussed life and everything from politics to literature and God to children. I had to remind myself that he was only 25 – he was a real old soul at heart. The chemistry and understanding was more than a match for the imbalance in our years. I completely fell for him – it was like being 16 all over again. He had a way of being which resonated deep inside me. It was the silly little things that I found myself adoring the most – like watching and loving the way that one of his eyes almost closed when he smiled, that sort of thing.

But it's never good news when your heart is saying one thing and your head is telling you another. And while I thought, *You know, you probably shouldn't...*, my heart was thumping away loud enough to drown out the cautionary voice. Yet my heart won – as it always does. I spent the night with Mattia in his tiny apartment far away from the huge villa which had become my Morcote prison. That night was a fairy tale as Mattia made my body feel full of life again. I felt beautiful and sexy and I felt adored – it was just what I needed. And there were certain physical things about his stamina that were particularly welcome – I wasn't spending the night with some old dude, that's for sure! It wasn't just great in the moment, though, it was something that felt truly nourishing in every way. I hadn't expected that anything could feel so wonderfully intense so soon.

Raoul moved out of Morcote and I thought I would give the place another go, but the villa represented everything that had brought me to attempting suicide and I couldn't get past the fact. Dark shadows lay over each room and each brick contained a bad memory. When I was in the house on my own it was particularly bad; I was always convinced there was someone else in the house with me and continually had to check and recheck every room. This wasn't for me. I left the villa for the last time and checked into the hotel where Mattia worked.

At last I felt safe and it was a pleasant novelty to be living full-time in a hotel. There was no fear here that we might be found. The hotel screened my calls and the manager reassured me that nobody would get to my door if I didn't want them to; that was what I needed to hear at that point.

Best of all I had my young, handsome lover close at hand: Mattia spent all his free time with me.

It wasn't until the divorce was over that I moved and we went to Milan, where I thought the kids could be well educated. My lawyer found me the perfect apartment in the San Siro area and I celebrated on the night before I checked out of the hotel by having a meal with Mattia. I had come to a decision.

'I'm crazy about you and I think we can have a great life together,' I told him. 'However, I need to be in Milan and if you can't move there with me, I don't know what we can do. It's been fun but now we need to think about whether we're going to be serious about this. After all these years I've run out of patience. I need an answer. I don't want to pressurise you, but I have to move on with my life and I can't do a long-distance thing or something that isn't for real.'

I meant it, but I also knew it was a tough ask. Mattia had a good set-up: he was enjoying the carefree life of a young bachelor in Switzerland and I wanted to rip him out of that. What did I have to offer him? I wasn't exactly over-the-hill yet but I was a mother of four with a lot of emotional baggage. I had set out the options but I really didn't know how he was going to answer. The only thing I was sure of was that I wasn't prepared to compromise and I wasn't going to put myself through the trauma of trying to make a relationship work between two countries with a guy in the prime of his life who worked in a hotel stuffed full of attractive young ladies. I wasn't stupid!

Mattia lay very quietly for a while, then he gently framed my face with his hands and looked straight into my eyes.

'Gitte, I'm crazy about you too,' he said, 'and I think we can have something really wonderful together. However... I can't live with a woman who smokes like a chimney and drinks far too much.' I was astonished.

I'd thought at first that he was going to agree without thinking about it or even say that he couldn't be with an older woman or didn't want to commit; something like that. But, despite his youth, he had again got right to the heart of things: he'd totally got the measure of me in that short time. What went unsaid about me had not gone unnoticed by him; he had my attention.

I felt very naked and yet it was how I knew he cared about me. If he hadn't have done, he wouldn't have mentioned the booze. It was a long time since anyone around me – friends or family – had shown such interest in my well-being that they were willing to stop tip-toeing around and tell it to me like it was.

Love should be unconditional if it is to be real, but Mattia was smart enough to set out the rules before he let himself go. I was a great woman, but I was a woman with problems and more issues than you could ever imagine – and there were likely to be more to come, but he was willing to deal with that if I was, too. Be honest, he was saying. Are you going to fix yourself or not? If you aren't gonna do it then I can't follow you. This was my wake-up call and now I had to make it happen.

CHAPTER 23

COMEBACK TO REALITY

When Mattia arrived in Milan looking nervous and ill at ease I was immediately on edge. I was very happy with him and I wondered what was about to happen so I asked him what was going on. 'I'm sick and tired of doing that commute between Switzerland and Italy...' he began. I was relieved that was all that bothered him. And he was right – he'd been living out of suitcases for months. Our relationship was still new enough for me to feel tingly and jumpy whenever we discussed things and I didn't know how I would have taken it if he'd have been sick and tired of us together.

'...so I resigned today. I'm ready to move in with you,' he went on. 'If that's okay with you?' Of course it was okay! It was more than okay, it was outrageous, wonderful and it was just... fucking great! Ever since then we have been inseparable.

Mattia is my best friend, my lover and he's a friend to my

kids. I wouldn't just call him a step-dad. He's my partner in crime and he manages some of my work for me too, a little bit of everything. Things are completely different now: Mattia won't have me out doing any old job but makes sure that it works for me as much creatively as it does in the business sense. I've found myself turning down things that, without thinking, I might have accepted before – Mattia makes me consider what I'm doing even if it's loads of money. He's never pushy, but he guides me in the right direction and it's worked out much better than I could ever have dreamed. Whether I'm working around the corner or on the other side of the planet he's more often than not with me and I feel safer for it. He always has his hand out – but to hold mine, not just to grab the cash.

My career began to pick up. *The Mole* had won a huge audience and its success and my honesty on screen hadn't gone unnoticed in the US, where reality TV was booming. Among the many offers I received was VH1's *Surreal Life*, which had built a big fan-base and was looking forward to its third series. The show was a little bit like a grander version of *Celebrity Big Brother*. Eight celebrities were picked to live in a luxurious house with a well-stocked bar in the Hollywood Hills. There was the usual assortment of challenges and activities to keep the participants busy but unlike *Big Brother*, there was no obligation to do anything. That sounded just perfect and it was a good excuse for getting back to LA: I might have left the city 20 years earlier but I still felt like we had a long-distance relationship and my love remained. The financial rewards were also attractive as I needed to make up for everything I'd given up in the divorce.

The producer wouldn't tell me who would be sharing the house but he did encourage me to think of something 'spectacular' to mark my arrival. The whole concept of reality TV struck me as being really silly and I wanted to have fun with it. It didn't occur to me at the time that I would be looked down on for doing that kind of thing and it would affect my chances of getting movie roles. I threw myself into the spirit of the thing and selected the tightest, most fabulous Gianni Versace dress – one that was given to me towards the end of my career as a model – with a pair of high heels. Instead of booking a limo I freaked everyone out by going back to my roots and riding a horse bareback to the house in all my finery.

I stepped into the house, smiling at the thought of being back in the US, far away from everything I knew again. None of the other seven faces looked remotely familiar to me, but I had been in Europe for a long time and hadn't really been keeping up with trends in the States. There was a flamboyant Spanish entertained called Charo, stand-up comedian and actor Dave Coulier, Public Enemy rapper Flavor Flav, New Kids on the Block singer Jordan Knight and the beautiful *American Idol* performer Ryan Starr. Our task over the next couple of weeks was nothing harder than to get to know one another and hang out.

Flavor Flav took an instant dislike to me. He kept looking me up and down, his every gesture conveying contempt. He was black, he was short and he was very unfriendly. I decided that I wasn't going to ignore his attitude and straight off said, 'Who the fuck are you?' This made him angrier and nervous too. I don't think he expected me to come back so aggressively. He backed out of the room, me following him, until he was right up against a wall. We faced each other, him looking up, me staring down at him from a height accentuated by my heels. There was a silence as we had a stare-out competition to decide who could show they gave less of a shit about the other. He had his gold teeth and jewellery, I had my little evening bag, and when this rude little man's attitude got too much I slapped him across the face with it.

He totally lost it. 'You lanky, skinny, ugly *bitch*!' he yelled. 'No one touches me, no one hits me in my face. You understand that, you motherfucker?' He was all over the place. Later he would confide in me that as a result of bad experiences he'd had as a child he just couldn't deal with anyone touching his face, much less hitting him.

'Fair enough,' I said in response to his outburst. 'I won't hit you, but you need to start respecting me and just cool that attitude of yours. Just stop with the theatrics, it's horrible.'

'Yeah, I'll stop that,' he said. With that we simultaneously collapsed into laughter, sat down together and started talking properly. And that was how I met William Jonathan Drayton Jr, aka Flavor Flav, a man who became as intimate a friend over the next couple of weeks as it was possible to be without me being unfaithful to Mattia.

Talk about the odd couple. Many people would have said that this rapper was too much caught up in his Public Enemy image, too angry and too anti-white to be friendly with me. The race question was all-consuming for Flavor Flav – or 'Foofie Foofie', as I ended up calling him, much to his pretended outrage. Public Enemy were militant in lyrical imagery about their struggle with white people. Foofie saw a towering blonde Caucasian woman enter the house and to him I represented everything this racially-obsessed man hated. Anyone would have said that the chances of the two of us becoming soul mates were zero.

As time passed, the uptight persona that Foofie presented was softened. 'Get over it!' I'd tell him. 'I'm white – and so what? You might be angry with a lot of white people but right now you're talking to me. We're not all the way you think of us.'

I guess that he came to listen to my point of view and I know that he loved the way I called him William rather than Flavor Flav. His name reminded me of an Italian ad for mattresses featuring an elephant named Foofie Foofie, the nearest translation for his stage name. Our conversations in the house would come to include his time in jail, his relationship with his ex-wife and the many children and lovers that he had. I talked about my marriage to Raoul and everything else that you've been reading about in this book. Opposites attract, but the sort of problems we faced and the pain we've felt was very similar. It got to the point where the producers had to remind us that there were other people in the house too. There was still a show! Please, mingle! We couldn't just carry on as if nobody else was there, we would end up stealing the show – which was what happened as things got so intimate the next step would have been sexual. It never happened, although we shared a bed and I couldn't deny the warm feelings I had for Foofie, but I couldn't do it because I was so in love with Mattia. And besides, Foofie is one ugly motherfucker.

Nevertheless, it was still hard for Mattia to watch what was going on. Fortunately, we had a lot of down-time on the show and they let us use the phone. I would spend hours talking to him in Italy and that meant he never felt left out. It was so odd for me to feel my love for Mattia grow at the same time as I was having such a close relationship with Foofie; work had crossed into genuine emotion. Yet Mattia was loyal and showed his love by backing me all the way and understanding that I was impulsive but that I would respect the boundaries. It was, even so, a very tough time.

The audience couldn't believe what they were seeing, not least because inter-racial relationships are still contentious in the US. Seeing this platonic love affair on-screen, with me and Foofie rolling around for the cameras, was a real eye-opener. The other contestants became extras with us as the main attraction and when we weren't centre stage, I would be keeping everyone entertained by taking over bar duties. If I wasn't fooling with Foofie, talking with Mattia or asleep I would be having an intense relationship with a bottle of Jack Daniel's. My antics ensured I was a big hit with everyone, particularly when I got so drunk I fell off my bar stool. Or I'd be jumping and dancing tipsily around the house on my own. The viewers loved the way I didn't hide anything but much later when I went into rehab the staff showed me clips of *Surreal Life* by way of telling me that, yes, I had a good time but look how I behaved.

Foofie and I worked so well together that VH1 commissioned a special spin-off between the two of us and Mattia. I said it had to be called *Strange Love*. Over 12 episodes I was to date

Flavor – without anything happening between us – and marry Mattia at the end. I lived with Flavor in the Bronx for half of it and then he came and stayed with Mattia and me in Italy. The show was another hit, with VH1 viewers watching the surreal goings-on as we kissed, slept in the same bed and then went to stay with Mattia.

The producers came back with an offer for *Strange Love II*. They gave me a blank cheque and told me to name my price. It was just crazy but I'd had enough by then. I felt I'd got to understand so much about what Flavor Flav and other black people had suffered; I could empathise with why he hated the white race so much. But I'd tease him about his own ignorance and had seen the way we were in front of the cameras had stirred up controversy. Now it was time to move on.

It was good to be back in LA, though, and to have made a hit. We'd earned VH1 a ton of money and the result was that I had even more offers for follow-ups. I had conquered the town all over again, for the first time since the split from Sylvester. Millions of viewers had seen me and it felt good to be in the sort of hit I hadn't seen since I did the likes of *Beverly Hills Cop II* and *Cobra*, some 20 years earlier.

It might have been that show which brought me to the attention of UK reality TV producers. The makers of *Celebrity Big Brother* invited me over for what they said would be a fun experience. I didn't see why not: it was just something I did for the money, it didn't seem too demanding and you didn't need any talent to do it. You could use it to present yourself in a certain way if you wanted but I decided just to be me – no bullshit. I wasn't sure about spending another three weeks away from Mattia but they said there would be a house full of celebrities. As it turned out, everyone knew who I was while I didn't recognise any faces.

We got chatting and I got on with everyone apart from John McCririck. Not only did he have cold-sores on his lips, but he used the same handkerchief to dab at them all the time. Disgusting! We all had bunk beds as if we were back in summer camp and John's nightwear consisted of enormous grubby white underpants, which were frankly frightening. As if that wasn't gross enough, he farted all the time. It didn't take me long to realise that John was a real misogynist: his comments and the way he talked to the women in the house were really not at all okay.

Bez, the dancer from Happy Mondays, was really nice but very sweaty. He was in the bed above me and the sweat would drip through which made for a nice accompaniment to John's flapping pants. Bez was great, though: he went on to win the show and I was really pleased for him.

We were without our suitcases for the first 24 hours, which was a new test added to the show that year. I only had the clothes I'd come in wearing and no make-up so that was a scary experience for me that first morning. Aside from the few games that the producers got us to play there was little to do. As with *Surreal Life*, it was all really about how you got to know each other and how the relationships developed. For the most part the days really seemed to drag on. You weren't allowed to read or write anything but Mattia had given me a little keepsake with four pictures of the two of us and with the kids on holiday. Behind each one he had inscribed lines of romantic poetry and that was all that kept me going.

On the third day Big Brother announced that we had to go to the front door and line up. We were dressed as historical servants from a castle at the time. One of us was going to be the ruler. They told us that we were about to get a new housemate, which was exciting when we'd got so used to one another. We faced the door and I saw that there was a gap between the base and the floor; light for the cameras seeped under the door and I could make out a shadow of something coming. It looked rather like a cat and for a moment I wondered if they'd got us a pet.

The door opened and the light behind made it hard to work out what was there. It was clearly a person, but who? I could make out this tangled mass of hair and I saw that it was red. Then I heard the voice. 'It's Jackie!' I recognised the sound as Jackie Stallone but my mind didn't quite register that it really was her at first. She shuffled in through the fog and it was indeed Jackie, though to me she looked more like some kind of monster with the Vegas make-up, the strange mouth and the piles of hair. 'Brigitte!' she called when I greeted her. She went straight for me and we hugged, though I couldn't have seen her for more than 15 years. I just remembered how she had disliked me and hadn't come to the wedding. My legs felt a bit weak but when I really looked at her and saw that she didn't seem quite right, I felt sorry for her. 'Oh, you're going to be helping me out here,' she continued. 'I really don't know anyone.'

It was a really low blow for the producers to have done this to us – they were probably hoping for a fight. Jackie was made Queen of the *Big Brother* house and we had to clean up after her. After all the bad feeling the last thing I wanted to do was be her servant but I had to deal with the situation as it was. She had to be about 80 by now, I thought, and our relationship was a long time in the past. She unpacked in the double bedroom she'd been allocated and told me that she needed her Scotch nightcap before bed. I stopped her mid-flow.

'You have to understand, Jackie, there are cameras all around us.'

'Cameras? I can't see any cameras.'

'No, that's just it, they're behind all the mirrors and the fittings.'

She started to pick away at her hair until the strands of red were everywhere and then she began to get undressed. I tried again. '*Jackie*! Don't do that here. You're in front of TV cameras.' Later on I took it up with Big Brother themselves in the Diary Room, telling them that it wasn't fair and they weren't unleashing similar surprises on anyone else. I had debated with myself as to whether or not I should leave, but decided that was childish and I had to deal with it.

Jackie told me she didn't know how to cook and that she couldn't even boil an egg for herself. I ended up taking care of her. We talked about Sylvester and she basically apologised, saying she realised that things had simply never been meant to be between the two of us. We started afresh together.

She went on to leave the house early – I don't know if that was part of the game or if she hadn't got something that she needed, but I felt good that there had been some kind of resolution between the two of us. You can make things better if you forgive people, I realised, and I even went to visit her at her home a couple of times after the show. The production didn't get the fireworks they might have wished for.

People at home must have liked me because I ended up staying the whole three weeks and when I did come out, I found that they were really friendly, having seen me at my rawest in there. I'd actually hoped that I would be voted off as it really wasn't my thing, but I was there on the very last night and I was the third from last out. They did ask me to come back for the final series in the summer of 2010 but I had decided it wasn't something I wanted to repeat.

If nothing else, *Big Brother* meant that I didn't drink for three weeks and I didn't really miss it. I did become convinced that Mattia would have decided to move on by the time I got out, though, but he was still there. We were stronger as a couple than ever, but we were going to need to be to face the challenges that lay ahead. My newfound success in reality TV had brought its own set of problems.

We had to face the fact that in order to capitalise on all the shows I was doing I had to base myself in LA. If I was going to do that then I wasn't sure I could uproot the kids from Milan and that felt really dreadful: life had been so good in Italy. We had moved into a great house and Mattia was by my side, but you can't be part-time in LA in the way that you can commute between Italy and London and I didn't have the physical endurance that I had at 20 to deal with jetlag.

It was such a hard decision to make and often I had tears in my eyes as I thought through all the options. I couldn't take the boys out of school and make them start all over again in LA. They would be away from Raoul and would have to learn a new language. Mattia and I knew we would be coming back on a regular basis and although the schools had amazing facilities in the US that made the most of the Californian climate, Los Angeles wasn't the best city to bring up young kids. Yes, I had friends and connections and could make it comfortable for them, but I thought it was too selfish to yank them out of the lives they had become used to. After all our research and planning I spoke to Douglas and Raoulino, who both had good friends in school they didn't want to lose. I knew we were doing the right thing.

In 2007 I got on the plane for the last time as a resident of Italy. We'd had been commuting by air since 2004 without committing to a new life. This was it – we were doing it. Was this to be the beginning of a new life? Perhaps I was returning to what I'd left when I went into exile 20 years ago...

CHAPTER 24

DETOX AND REHAB

I missed my children in LA. The guilt I felt about leaving them behind in Italy made me drink even more, too. Mattia and I had moved into a beautiful home in the Hollywood Hills but my routine had got as bad as it had been in Morcote. Every day the half-drunk and the fresh bottles would come out of their hiding places all over the house. There were no longer any gaps between my sessions and it was beginning to take its toll, but there was a difference between Morcote and here in the Hollywood Hills: Mattia.

'You are destroying yourself,' he told me. 'It cuts me up to see you like this. You *have* to do something before you kill yourself. And if you don't get help then I am going to leave you.' It sounded tough, but Mattia's approach was so much more constructive than Raoul's. He cared but he let me know that he was serious. I had considered seeing someone back in Lugano but I'd just thrown the contact details away. Now I could see the truth: I was probably more of an alcoholic than I had been when I tried to kill myself.

'Of course, Mattia,' I said. 'I promise you I'll never touch another drop, honestly.' And I was dry for three weeks. I didn't even feel like drinking, I was fine, but when he had to go out unexpectedly one morning on an errand I found a bottle from my secret stash and even though I didn't want to disappoint him, I drank behind his back. There were occasions when I couldn't manage without it – talking to my mother on the phone or dealing with important stuff for the kids. I believed I could bluff my way through without anyone finding out and I stumbled on for another six months. Sometimes Mattia would find a bottle and then we'd start the whole charade again. I wasn't fooling anyone: it was an absolute nightmare of a life but nobody could help me – and I certainly couldn't help myself – until I laid my cards on the table and faced the truth.

I can't remember the date when everything finally came to a head, but I can tell you the day was a Thursday. 'You need professional help,' said Mattia again. 'If not, we're through right now. I can't live with someone who drinks as much as you.' I knew that I had lied so much and abused his trust to such a degree that he might never believe me again; I was in despair.

Desperately, I called him all the names under the sun and screamed, 'Let me fucking drink! You can't stop me. I'm going to fucking drink and if you can't fucking handle it, why don't you just fuck off?' Inside, of course, I didn't want him to go – I wanted him to save me – and that's what he did. He got me to admit that I was about to throw everything away.

In my head I never thought of drinking as being so damaging; I had always thought of it as something I did rather than something I was. An actual alcoholic, I believed, was someone else. They were smelly, shaky, forgetful and they would throw up after their sessions, but now I realised that I *was* an alcoholic. That was me. And Mattia had the right to call me that. This was my last chance.

When he went out to the shops I thought to myself, *This is it – it's now or never*. I turned on the computer and nervously opened up a browser window. I got to a search engine and as I began to cry, I typed in 'rehab' and 'Los Angeles', then I gazed at the results and decided on one because of its name. I'm not going to say what the name of the place was because it's important to preserve confidentiality in respect of other patients and their treatment, but it was the name that attracted me. That sounds so banal, but through my tears and my feelings of helplessness there seemed no better way of doing things.

Feeling alone and scared, I dialled the number as I panicked about what sort of thing you should say in this kind of situation: 'Hello, my name is Gitte and I'm an alcoholic'. No – stupid. Perhaps I should make up a name. I couldn't deal with it so I hung up and went straight out of the house to the nearest shop and bought the first bottle of vodka I could find – I didn't care what kind or how much it was. I finished half the bottle before going back to the phone and dialling the number again as the vodka hit my system and I began to feel a little lighter and safer.

'Hello. Who am I speaking with and how can I help you?' The voice was female, friendly but steady. Oh God, so I did have to say who I was. I'll hang up – it'll get into the press. I can't do it. The receiver stayed pressed against my ear.

'It's Brigitte,' I whispered. 'I drink too much.' I sounded incoherent through my tears.

'Sorry, Brigitte?' she asked. 'Is that your full name?'

'No. It's Brigitte Nielsen.'

'Okay. I can hear you're very, very sad. How do you feel?' Now I really started crying – it was as if someone had just that moment hit me hard. It was a release and my defences collapsed. 'Calm down, Brigitte, it's okay. Take your time... do you live with anyone?'

'My boyfriend.'

'Great! That's really good. You're happy together?'

'Yes,' I said, 'but he hates the fact that I drink.'

'Good,' she said. 'That's why you called the right people. I'm glad you did. Pack a bag right now and tomorrow morning you are going to drive here with your boyfriend and check-in.' The decision had been made and although I felt a spasm of terror at what might happen next, it did seem as if it might be all right. As I continued crying she went on, 'So you think you drink too much. Do you think you are an alcoholic?' Her voice never sounded any less friendly.

'Yes,' I said. 'I think I have become an alcoholic.'

'You *think* that's what you've become?' She continued in a measured tone which gave me time to recover my composure, 'Don't be afraid and most of all, don't be embarrassed – there are so many people like you with us and even more out there who haven't yet called us. We won't do anything difficult tomorrow: we'll have a chat with you and your boyfriend and just find out how we might be able to help you.' I wasn't made to feel guilty or sneaky and worthless: I was just another person who needed help.

Mattia and I were both in tears as we set off for the clinic – I was anxious about going, while he was happy that I was finally doing something about my condition. This was the last bit of the baggage I had been carrying from my marriage to Raoul.

The woman who spoke to me on the phone greeted us, we signed off on some paperwork and that was it – I was in that Friday. I wasn't allowed any outside contact for the first two weeks of my stay. It felt as if I had been sent to prison – and that wasn't so far from the truth. My random choice of rehab wasn't one of the fancy clinics with relaxed, spa-like regimes, good views and discreet staff to wait on you. It was more commonly used as the place of last resort for women who would otherwise be in a real prison. Often they were there for anything from six to 18 months – it was meant for those with heavy duty problems.

The reception area had been a welcoming area like a private hospital with flowers and comfortable seating. Then I was led away on my own through what was probably part of the residential area to a serious-looking set of doors which locked shut behind us. Through those doors the building looked somewhere between a medical facility and a secure institution. Was this really the right place for me? Perhaps they'd misunderstood me – I was a drinker, not a murderer! But while glamorous rehabs might have been more luxurious, they also had a far higher rate of clients going back to their addiction. I later found out that I had picked the strictest centre in all of California and it had the greatest success in getting people off drugs.

The first five days were incredibly hard. To begin with I was happy: I wanted to get myself free of alcohol with every fibre of my body. They gave me Valium to relax and the toxins began to be released; they told me not to try and keep to a routine for the next couple of days but just to let myself go with the process. Meanwhile, they looked after me and kept a constant medical check on how my organs were functioning. I was encouraged to eat as much as I could to build up my strength for the treatments which lay ahead, all of which sounded rather ominous.

I wasn't in too bad shape. My body hadn't been as poisoned as it might have been and I didn't suffer any physical withdrawal effects: the effect on me was all psychological. Around me was the constant screaming of the narcos, the girls who were coming off heroin and other hardcore drugs. It was a section of society which I'd never encountered before and frequently very frightening. However bad things were for me I knew that I was still lucky not to be like them.

I should say that in writing this I don't want to scare anyone off from going into rehab: I didn't know how tough the regime was going to be and later I got some respectful nods from top doctors when they found out that I had done so voluntarily. Reading about it may seem daunting, but if you're suffering from addiction I can promise you their programme is nothing worse than where you are coming from. There's nothing to be afraid of, but I do want to give an idea of what it was like in there.

The clinic had a postage stamp-sized outside area which was the only place you could go for fresh air or to have a cigarette. We were like animals held in a small enclosure at the zoo. Some of the other women looked so close to death that if they made it through treatment, it was obvious they wouldn't see their next birthday. That was a wake-up call for me – I felt I was on the same road. Those who were doing heroin and other substances died so much more quickly than many alcoholics. The memories of the people I met there will always be imprinted in my mind.

I was issued with a military-style blanket to sleep under and at 7am on the dot we all had five minutes to jump out of bed, make it, get dressed and have our shoes out from under the bed and on. Our closet areas had to be clean enough to pass a thorough daily inspection and we then waited to be taken to breakfast. It was served in the cafeteria, where we lined up with a tray before eating in total silence. Though the Valium helped me sleep, my nights were disturbed by the screams of the three girls who shared the room with me. It was like being in an asylum. They would do strange things and I was constantly worried that they would attack me or the staff.

The days passed monotonously: I began to eat small amounts of food along with the drugs that I guess were used to flush out my system. I felt sorry for myself all over again – I had time to ask myself how I had ended up there – and that was really the start of my treatment. One of the other patients I talked to was a young guy who had been on drugs for as long as he could remember. He freaked out when his mother died and ended up in treatment. His father was never around but he was a really nice boy and I got to know quite a lot about him. Three months after I left the rehab he died of an overdose: he was 22.

My Valium was withdrawn after those first five days, but I was still not permitted any contact with the outside world – not even with Mattia. I was tired of the whole thing, it was ridiculous. I'd been doing really well surrounded by all these crazy people and they still wouldn't even allow me five minutes with Mattia; I was sure I didn't need to stay there any longer.

'You're free to go any time you want,' they said, 'but if you leave before your treatment is finished then your insurance won't cover it.'

'I don't care – I need to go, I'm over it. There are too many people here and I can't adapt to this way of life. They're criminals – murderers, drug users. They're ten times worse than me!'

'Of course, Brigitte,' they said. 'If that's what you want to do. Go ahead and do your thing. Try not to misuse alcohol again and remember about the insurance. And, by the way, if you leave under these circumstances you can never come back again.' It was said politely but very firmly and I knew that they meant it. I stayed.

The first task each day after breakfast was to clean the bathrooms and the kitchens, wash the floors, wipe the windows and tidy up the communal areas. People who had been there the longest got to allocate the tasks, the worst of which was the bathrooms. With a pair of heavy rubber gloves on I would get down on my knees in the showers and as I scrubbed at the shit and vomit, I would think back to my million-dollar home in the Hollywood Hills. All the high points of my life flashed in front of me as I tried to get rid of the stench – the marriage to Sylvester, the movies, the albums... whatever.

Mornings continued with a 12-step plan meeting, the system for recovering users made famous by Alcoholics Anonymous. We discussed our thoughts in a group and shared progress in our treatment. While some of it was helpful for me, I didn't get along with the way it seemed to cover every last aspect of your life. It might be perfect for a lot of people but for me it had overtones of brainwashing. These days I don't go to AA meetings as many times as it was suggested I should, but I realised then – and I still know it now – that I was a user and I will remain one for the rest of my life.

Specialist doctors would say that it's part of the sickness that I would prefer to have dinner with Mattia than go to nightly AA meetings, but I couldn't do it. Yet the sessions did provide the tools to make me sure my life won't get stuck again. I guess what I'm saying here to people who have faced similar situations is that you have to find your own way – listen to what they say in rehab, but whatever you do – go for it.

Lunch would be followed by gruelling sessions with a psychiatrist and while we weren't allowed to listen to music or watch TV there were occasionally movies. Anyone hoping for escapism would be disappointed as it would always be a documentary about alcoholism or drug use.

I was assigned a case worker, who kept detailed notes of every conversation we had. She was always very frank with me when she assessed how long she thought I would be staying in the clinic. I found it all very depressing: every day followed the same routine. Back in the dorm room one of the girls would be sitting on her bed staring vacantly into space; another would be crying out in her sleep. It was relentless and it was devastating to see girls 20 years younger than me look as if they were completely done. I said to myself, 'Take a good look around you, Gitte. Thank God you got help in time.' And to think I hadn't wanted to do it.

The biggest crisis I faced during my stay was on my birthday: I was frightened, lonely and miserable. I begged them to let me have just a five-minute call with Mattia. Even 30 seconds hearing his voice would have made everything seem okay.

'There's a phone box on the other side of the street,' they said. 'You can use that – but when you walk out and close the door you aren't coming back. If you feel you need to call him, then you have to forget about what you're doing here.' My 43rd birthday was spent with desperately ill alcoholics listening to the constant, strange wailing of the narcos; that was the worst. I don't know what it was, whether it was something they'd taken with their heroin, but they never stopped yelling.

Perhaps because I was in better shape I became a focal point for the treatment group. I don't want to say I was a leader, but I sort of carried them with me. That opened up something in me as I was able to compare my own, terrible stories with those that were often far worse. We were all really fucked up but they also supported me too. The biggest difference between us was that almost all of them had nowhere to go when they were done with their treatment at the centre. No friends, no family. When things got tough for me I would tell myself that if I couldn't make it in here, I might as well lie down and die because I had Mattia, my kids, my mother and my girlfriends all waiting for me.

The other women could only look forward to getting out to be greeted by the men who wanted to get them into prostitution, get them back on drugs and use them to do crime. Most of them had children of their own by the time they were 16. I thought about my own unhappiness as a child and how privileged I'd been in reality. There I was saying how terrible it was to be laughed at as a kid and how that had thrown a shadow over my life, but there was really no comparison to what these girls endured. Not surprisingly, as the others there began to get clearer, they wanted to stay in the clinic for as long as possible. There they were safe, but there was nothing provided on the outside.

In meetings with the psychiatrist I explored what had gone wrong for me but I didn't find it easy to open up – I think my fear was all about this being the first time that I had really been worked on to let out my demons. I was allowed the time to let go without the feeling that there were always people watching what I was doing. The exercises included writing a farewell letter to my father and another to my sickness. I decided to address that one personally to a bottle of Jack Daniel's:

To Jack and all the members of your family,

We have been friends for a very long time and you have always loved me with all your heart. You have a lot of patience. But you know I'm an honest person and I have to tell you that our relationship has to end right now due to personal reasons and very serious concerns for my health. I'm sure that you, with your great personality, power and good looks, will find new friends very, very soon.

The staff at the clinic patiently worked to untangle the knot in my stomach. And even though I found many of the sessions to be hard work, I really wanted to succeed. It wouldn't have happened any other way; I couldn't have resisted the treatment and kept sober.

Now I don't think I'll have to see a psychiatrist for the rest of my life but I know that the AA meetings will be a constant if occasional presence. It's so helpful to have other people to talk to about my problems and the future. Besides, I love to hear other stories and to learn about the situations that people have found themselves in. It helps to broaden my own perspective and it will always be important for me to think about what I am, even though I haven't drunk anything since 2007. I still think about it every day and I have slipped a couple of times, but even when I do, it doesn't mean the work I do on myself isn't still meaningful or that I won't reach a solution. My problem will always be a part of my life and I will always be aware of it.

CHAPTER 25

THE LAST HURDLE

The 14 days I spent in treatment felt more like 14 years. Even then I knew that the process of getting clean had only just begun and that I would have to watch myself carefully when I left. The treatment was supposed to take three months but even though they warned against thinking about life outside, I had work to do.

I was beginning to question all my assumptions about myself. Have you ever thought that the person you have to spend the longest time with is yourself? There will never be anyone closer to you than you are to yourself, but can you honestly say you're your own best friend? Do you talk to yourself every day? Do you know yourself as well as you should? Probably not. There are few of us who can talk about who we really are. Those were the thoughts that occupied me when I left.

In my marriage I had been my own worst enemy: I didn't listen to myself and I didn't support myself when I needed to. It was only me that could do it and it was only me who made sure it didn't happen. I got frustrated with myself, I blamed myself for not doing more and I was never sympathetic in the way I would have been had I been talking to a friend about her own problems.

When I thought about it I had to admit that I had never really been good to myself: we let ourselves down before we let anyone else down. In the end it got so bad for me that I almost lost everything. It might sound as if I think I know it all now, but that's the only way I can explain what happened to me.

If we want to live in harmony with ourselves, we need to find out who we are. You have to be painfully honest with yourself, you have to have the guts to look at who you really are rather than the person you would like to be. Can you list your own strengths and weaknesses and allow yourself to say them out loud to yourself? You have to stand by each aspect of your character, no matter what happens. That's what I mean when I say you need to be your own best friend.

When I came out I had to admit that I had no idea who I was or how I felt. Given that, there was no way I could look after myself – that's why I didn't have the strength and wisdom to know when to have fun and when to stop. I felt as raw as if layers of me had been peeled away, but I knew what my responsibilities were and that the next stage was to act on them. I would need help because I was, deep down, unhappy and I knew my cravings for alcohol wouldn't disappear just like that.

I faced my first major test the day I left. Foofie Foofie – aka Flavor Flav – had asked me to be a guest on *The*

Comedy Roast. This was the Comedy Central programme that affectionately mocked its stars and because we'd got on so well, Foofie had asked me to sit on the panel alongside the likes of Snoop Doggy Dogg, Ice-T and assorted comedians. The shows always descended into the meanest digs you could imagine. It was great fun to be part of it, to see Foofie again and to meet his friends, but there was also an uncomfortable side of it for me, being surrounded by drink and everyone trying to get me to take part. 'Hey Foofie, I've just literally yesterday got out of rehab,' I told him. They all congratulated me but within minutes I was being offered alcohol. 'No, thanks, I don't want to get back into that again.' I wasn't angry so much as disappointed. Were they really my friends? I wasn't suggesting that they didn't drink, but I didn't expect them to tempt me off the wagon.

That said, it was much easier to be open about going to rehab in the US. Celebrities were more proud of doing it than their equivalents in Europe. There was also no shame in failing and having to try again – some American stars are in and out for years. But in Italy you'd be far more likely to enjoy a glass of wine at 11 o'clock in the morning than you would worry about whether that made you an alcoholic.

The Comedy Roast seemed to go on forever and everyone had a drink in their hand all night long. Snoop was even smoking joints on the stage – which caused some controversy when it was reported the next day. I had a good evening though, sat there with my fizzy soft drink, but it opened my eyes to how many times I would have to face similar situations in everyday life. In those first few days I worried that I wouldn't always be strong enough to say

'No'. I resolved to check back into rehab the next weekend because I just didn't feel ready to face the world.

That same week my agent told me VH1 were doing a reality show called *Celebrity Rehab*. I would be treated by Dr Drew Pinsky, a top specialist in substance abuse and even better, I would get paid for it. It was the perfect opportunity. I wasn't in the slightest bit concerned about having my recovery filmed – I had lived so much of my life in front of the cameras by then. I had gotten drunk and acted like a fool on reality TV so I was certainly ready to set a better example for the viewers. There was opposition from those who felt that the whole idea behind Alcoholics Anonymous was that it was done in private, but I thought all of that was probably unnecessary. I passionately believed that you've got to show the world that it could happen to anyone, no matter who they are. Just as you might show the effects of war on television, you should show recovering addicts – you want to say, 'This is what it fucking looks like': you have to understand it.

Within days the contracts were agreed and I couldn't believe how lucky I'd been when I was all ready to go back to be treated under my own steam. I was to be the only one on the show who had previously been in rehab and I was the only one who went in sober; that didn't really fit with the concept and I was asked if I could look a bit woozy to begin with, which was fine. It was kind of fun in a way and though I worked hard at going through my alcoholism, the show was much milder than anything I'd experienced myself. The alcoholic I'd become was finally replaced by the woman I'm now only finally getting to know.

The programme was filmed in a wing at a real-life clinic called the Pasadena Recovery Center rather than in a studio. Just the other side of the wall from us would have been the same mix of real clients that I'd met myself. Unlike them we were allowed to use the phone for an hour and a half every day and we had our own food brought in. We didn't have to do any of the chores and we each knew that outside we had a world that we belonged in. Though all of us had unenviable stories, we also had careers and a network to support us afterwards and we weren't just left to fend for ourselves like those girls whose situation had shocked me so much in LA.

I shared a room with Chyna, an actress who had formerly been a pro-wrestler. Popular in the US, she was also very pretty in her own muscular way. She had been a *Playboy* centrefold but her life had got very crazy in recent years. In 2004, she and her then-boyfriend made a sex video inevitably called *One Night in Chyna*. She misused pills and alcohol but what made her unique in the show was her denial. Until almost the last day she insisted she didn't know why she was there. She had been physically abused, she drank too much and she was a cutter – she self-harmed – and she didn't want to admit to it. Dr Drew also said she was had bipolar disorder (the condition formerly known as manic depression). Even when she did finally admit that she had a problem she wasn't able to say what it was. I've often wondered what happened to her – I later read that she had been taken to hospital after an overdose.

Daniel Baldwin, one of the four acting brothers, left after just a couple of days and Jeff Conaway – who played

Kenickie in *Grease* – talked about leaving every day but never did. He was probably the sickest one of us all and was twice rushed to hospital during filming. It's easy to judge people but harder to work out how they end up in such situations.

Mary Carey was a porn star who essentially showed up in a coma, thanks to a cocktail of pills similar to the one that killed Heath Ledger. She came out of it during the show but went straight back into the same world afterwards to make *Celebrity Pornhab with Dr Screw*.

American Idol singer Jessica Sierra had never forgiven her mother for dying of an overdose, but she was one of the few to get completely clean after the show and she's since returned to singing. I felt I was able to talk to her as someone who had tried to take the overdose way out. 'It's not because your mother didn't love you,' I said. 'Mothers always love their children but we get lost – that's what addiction does to you. You take the bottle over your kids.'

Child star Jaimee Foxworth and Crazy Town singer Seth Binzer were also on the show. Seth was so much the archetypal wild man of rock that I could never imagine him getting completely sober – it'd be like telling Keith Richards in his 1970s pomp that he should really go and get himself straight. Jaimee got clean in the end and has more recently had a child.

Ricco Rodriguez was a martial arts champion who also got clean.

Some of the participants had stories which made mine look like a walk in the park. I was fresh from a rigorous regime and my head was just in a different place; I felt stronger and I also knew that I wanted it one hundred per cent. Very quickly, I became the group's mother figure and though it was hard to hear all the awful testimony, I realised that I had a lot to be grateful for. I was all the more determined not to throw it away by going back to drinking.

My biggest challenge was living away from home without my boys and Mattia. We spoke every day and the producers organised a family day, which kept us going. There was a lot of criticism for the way the show used the stars' misfortunes for sensationalistic effect. I didn't agree. Personally, I got a lot out of the show at a time when I really was giving myself one last chance to get better and I felt that under Drew Pinsky I was in the safest pair of hands the programme makers could have found. It wasn't exploitative just because there were cameras there. The US needed a show like *Celebrity Rehab* to start a discussion between young people and their parents about substance abuse. We could do with more of that in Europe as well: there should be more done about alcoholism by the media, schools and authority. It's a problem in the UK and it's even worse in my home country of Denmark. I only wish that something like *Celebrity Rehab* had been around when my modelling friend Gia was getting into the heroin use which would see her die of AIDS. Perhaps if addiction hadn't been taboo she would still be around today.

After only six weeks I was released to be met by Mattia, Killian, Douglas and Raoulino. The boys all said how proud they were that I had got myself sober. We hugged and I felt that deep inside me a new person was beginning to grow. It was one of the happiest moments of my life and

I doubt there is a better feeling than that of knowing your children respect what you've done. I was overwhelmed with love for them and that in itself provided me with a vital defence against the alcoholism. There were so many reasons to keep away from drink, but I didn't need anything more than them.

Dr Drew said that I needed to pay close attention to the environment in which I was living so Mattia and I sat down to make an ambitious plan to change our lives: we wanted to design a programme that would minimise my chances of relapsing. The most important move was to get out of Los Angeles, the city of sin, for a while and relocate to the sunshine of Palm Springs, some 180 kilometres away. It was known for its fitness centres and health resources – exactly the opposite of LA. The pace of life was much more relaxed there and there weren't so many liquor stores to tempt me away from my intended path.

In 2007 we made the move and I completely altered my daily routine. I kept off the drink, I gave up smoking and Mattia and I maintained a strenuous work-out. We became more interested in eating a healthy diet as well. After about a year we felt strong enough to move back to Los Angeles without succumbing to its temptations. We loved the city and it was still the only place to do business. You have to be available to do castings, which is now a little old-fashioned. In Europe everything's done off computer listings but I actually preferred to meet with people.

We took a really nice villa back in the Hollywood Hills. It's green and lovely out there but at the same time we had all the benefits of being close to the action. Studio City isn't far away and when I took the dogs out for a walk we could look over at the legendary house where Hitchcock filmed *Psycho*, the burned-out shell of *Airport* and the location of Clint Eastwood's *Pale Rider*.

Instead of having cocktail parties we concentrated on realising the creative ideas that we'd had together. I'd wasted so much time drinking over the years. Now I had even more energy than before I drank and I was in even more of a hurry with less than half of my life left to me.

We also had to cut down our social circle. Most evenings I would be on Skype with my kids or settling down in front of the TV. I'm a documentary freak and it was really important to me to record the good shows. I was just a small fish in Hollywood – a *very* small fish – but it was still funny that every other day there would be something on a movie channel with me in it. I'd watch and marvel at how young I looked.

CHAPTER 26

WE LOVE YOU, MUM

B ob Marley's 'Could You Be Loved' was on the radio next to me. His gentle voice reminded me that when you point your finger at other people they do the same to you. I loved that song. Marley was my idol when I was 14 and I'm still crazy about his music and lyrics; they have something meaningful to say about society but also a sense of release about them too.

Outside the sun was high in a cloudless sky. The waves crashed onto the beach and the wind tickled the leaves in the trees. I was lying on a towel with my feet in the sand and next to me was a large glass of cold Coca-Cola without a drop of rum in it. I didn't have much difficulty keeping off the alcohol.

Mattia was playing with the kids in the water. They were getting silly and laughing together as they chased each other. I was proud that I was still able to be part of their world. When I was drunk I didn't notice the seasons pass or the birds flying high as I had done as a child. The sensations I felt on the beach in Jamaica that day seemed completely new.

Mattia and I had met the kids at Miami International, the third-largest airport in the US. It was the first time in almost a year that I'd seen Killian, Douglas and Raoulino but I couldn't remember ever feeling quite so excited; my heart was just about ready to bubble over with joy. It wasn't the first time I'd greeted them at an airport and with their father living in Milan, it wouldn't be the last – but I couldn't say when I'd last truly been Gitte. I couldn't wait for the boys to see their new, sober mummy. Usually I had been able to see them about four or five times a year: Easter, a month of holiday time, Christmas and then whenever I was in Europe. It was a good set-up. I had only gone longer this time because I needed to take that year out to get straight.

Our destination was a beach bungalow in Jamaica owned by a close girlfriend of mine. We were going to swim, chat and have fun for two weeks – which actually then stretched into a month. For once there was no programme to follow: we were just going to be a family.

'We've been here for hours!' I said to Mattia. 'I can't wait any longer.'

'They'll be here in five minutes,' he said, and he was right. There they were – running through the passport check which, as ever in the US, had taken ages. And they had grown so big and they were so great; it was wonderful to see them again. I screamed with delight and we ran towards each other as if we were in some old, sentimental movie. They had their rucksacks on and looked very grown-up. All of them have become giants – Killian at 19 was a good couple of heads bigger than me, as he liked to point out. My other son, Julian, was 25 and lived between Copenhagen and London. It would have been wonderful to have had him with us in Jamaica, but we would still have an amazing time.

'We love you mummy!' they chorused. They were as happy as me that drink was no longer between us and we chattered excitedly, Douglas and Raoulino close to tears as the emotion got the better of them: they all knew how important this was. I could see myself in them when I was younger and now I could play an active part in watching them grow. I looked forward to playing on the beach with them, fixing their meals and waking them up in the morning.

It hadn't just been me I'd saved in rehab. Every kid in the world deserves to have parents who will always be there for them, to stand by their side and to inspire them. If I hadn't have been able to do that it would have left a lasting scar on my soul. I hope and I believe that I was in time to stop myself going too far.

I've had a great many narrow escapes in my life; I'd been thinking that as I flew to Miami with Mattia. We'd been in the UK, where I'd played the boss of a brothel for a production that took me a couple of days to film, typical of the sort of thing I was doing to make money. On the plane back, I remembered the ticket I'd booked for Pan Am Flight 103 from London to New York for 21 December 1988: I changed the reservation at the last moment and it was that flight which was blown up by a bomb over Lockerbie. Then on 8 October 2001 I was due to fly on SAS Flight 686 from Milan to Copenhagen and that plane hit a small private aircraft on the runway and everyone died. For me in recovery as an alcoholic it was another reminder of how much I had to feel lucky about. *Don't push your luck too much*, I thought as we flew.

The in-flight magazine had a picture of Michael Jackson on the front cover. It was a close-up dominated by his intense, dark eyes full of hurt. It seemed he was looking into my soul and I felt tears welling up. I knew Michael quite well when I was married to Sylvester and sometimes we'd met up since then, just chatting and on occasion even dancing together. I last saw him under sadder circumstances. We were in Modena in Italy for a charity concert given by our mutual friend Luciano Pavarotti. I was shocked when I saw Michael. He'd always been shy but happy and I remember him playing with Sylvester's dogs in the backyard or showing up at parties after concerts to have some fun. Since then the paedophile accusations had taken their toll and you could see how his plastic surgery was coming apart. His clumsy make-up was thickly applied to hide scars and the glue holding his wig on was obvious. He wore a hat that was battered and his trademark white gloves were dirty. When I heard about his death I remembered how he looked that last time and thought at least he was at peace, even though his children have lost a wonderful father.

Today I still find it hard to understand how I could have been so selfish and so far gone as to have believed that my own kids would have been better without their mother around. I thank God I've become wiser since then. Michael's tragically early death was more proof that I should never take life for granted.

I no longer believe that the grass is always greener, but that old saying sums up exactly how we spend most of our lives. Often we get distracted by little irritations and we find it hard to accept things as they are: there's always the new car, the bigger flat-screen and the more exotic holiday around the corner – if only we had the money for them. But would any of those things make us that much happier? And yet we pay for them even if we don't actually buy them through stressing out about how much we want them. That's already too great a cost. Do you recognise that scenario? I think most of us would, whereas what we should be doing is enjoying the journey we take in life.

As I write these words I'm thinking about all the years I spent trying to change the world around me, particularly when I was married to Raoul. I fought to become a good wife and mother but the family could never have been what I wanted it to be. The best thing I can do now is to leave that behind me. I don't try to alter or even to regret what has happened. Why worry about it?

Let me leave you with one last, irritating example of how people can be world-beaters at worrying about things that they can't do anything about. Whenever it rains in Denmark – and it rains a lot – people complain as much as they do in the UK, but we all know it rains all the time – because it just does. So we shouldn't worry – we need only to dig out our umbrellas and put them up. Embrace reality as it is – don't try to make it the way you want it to be. It's raining? Well, let it rain! The fundamental question is this – do you want to live in your own life or will you live in the world in which you regret your decisions and wish away your time in wanting things to change? Of course you should change what you can, but I'm just saying you shouldn't waste your mental energy trying to make changes where it's not possible.

A good exercise is to make a list of everything in your life that you wish was different. Count how many items there are. As a rule you'll have a handful. Cross out the ones you know that you'll never be able to change. Does that feel good? Now you'll be left with the things you can do. There's so much you can still achieve with your life, but it won't wait for you; it'll pass you by if you don't go for it. Prioritise and you'll find you can make a real difference to your little corner of the world.

Jamaica proved to be exactly the break that we needed. We had some great times together and that was so important – our family had lost so much time and we needed to catch up. The kids loved Mattia: he proved himself to be a real friend to them and they could see it. They called him Uncle Matt – *Onkel* in Danish. He had become part of the family but he never tried to replace their father and that was the way it should have been. It was the first time as an adult that I felt a sense of connectedness and family. We did all the ordinary stuff that makes life worth living – playing games, watching TV, eating together. It was all I really wanted. Nobody was being yelled at and nobody did any yelling.

We spent a lot of time just chatting about what we were

all doing with our lives, about girlfriends, about work. I wasn't the kind of mother who only wanted to know what their grades were: I was curious about what was on their iPods, what their favourite clothes were and where they liked to go out in the evening. As I asked I wondered what had really changed over the years – was it me, them or a mixture of everything? Now they weren't boys any more, they were young, handsome men and I wanted to be a part of the lives they were leading.

I can never let myself forget that another part of my own life is that I was, and I remain, an alcoholic. It's a chronic condition and one that I have to work on every day. I will even have to keep reminding myself when I'm at home in the Hollywood Hills: no more hectic barbecue parties in our garden for me, not even one glass of champagne when I'm at a reception – not any more. Not even when this book comes out. I will continue to go to AA meetings and if I feel I'm sliding, I will have to pick up myself up and keep going.

I had to leave many friends behind. Not because they were bad, but they just weren't a good influence for me in my new way of living. It used to be that I would be terrified about missing out on even one acquaintance in case that meant I ended up alone yet now I deleted a whole bunch of my Italian friends from my mobile. Today I am surrounded only by my real, true friends and family – and I would do anything for them. I knew I owed my life to them and one day maybe I can do something similar in return.

As my own boys grow up now I am also looking forward to seeing them get established in their own careers and maybe having children of their own. I think I'll be the world's best grandmother. I hope I could make grand-children feel as loved as I did by my own grandmother. I'll be there on the sidelines cheering them on in the good times and ready to offer my support when they're finding it tough. I want to repay those 10 years I lost conducting my affair with the bottle.

Finally, I would like to do something about those people who, 20 years after my divorce from Sylvester, still call me Gitte Stallone. They look at me as if I'm a cartoon character and they write me off as a hopeless actress. I want to fulfil the dreams I've had since I was at my school's concert playing at being Tina Turner. I'm so ready – I've never been more ready than I am now. I've got a good grasp of my priorities, I've made a plan and I'm sure I will reach some of my goals. I'm as excited as a kid on her way to Disneyland.

Raoulino was chasing Killian in the water while Mattia left the water to lie next to me. We talked about what I would do when I'm finished with the entertainment business. Perhaps we might start an exclusive restaurant in Thailand where we could spend time looking out over the sea in the sun. At that point it was enough that every day I lived I was getting further away from the nightmare I endured for so many years.

Mattia and the kids, not to say the rest of the world, would get used to Gitte in time. I was still working out how it felt to be her at last. Over the years I wasted so many business opportunities and I knew it would take a long time to rebuild that trust. I'd seen that it was easier to destroy relationships than to make everything right again: the most important thing to do was to forgive myself and thank God I've taken that step.

Today I think about Gitte, young and spontaneous, and I feel proud of her and her long, strange journey. She overcame all the tests that came her way and she faced her share of difficulties. I've met many interesting people, achieved a great deal and I've always persevered. I was one of the first Danish supermodels, I married a Hollywood superstar, I was a singer… I want to remember that I've had a great life, despite the many terrible times.

Best of all, of course, are the Four Musketeers – my kids. And not to forget my wonderful husband who I love and who adores me, even though I am always very conscious of the gap in our ages. I ignore what people say, but I know they all have their opinions. Sometimes I can't help feeling Mattia deserves better – I always feel like I have to be up-to-date and modern and it's very exhausting. I suppose I feel that he could do more with his life and I know that I come with a bagful of issues; I only hope that he isn't sacrificing too much for me – I don't want to have to feel guilty, but I do worry. He's living the life of me now, but when I was his age, wow! I had a very different agenda. Is that right? Well, it better be right, dammit!

Maybe I worry too much. Mattia doesn't like the limelight and he stays away from the camera whenever he can. He knows what he wants and he's pretty grounded, but I do think about ending up alone and frankly, it terrifies me. It's only me who sees this as a problem because he certainly doesn't. I talk about it all the time and he always reassures me. In fact, he gets sick of hearing about it.

One of the Jamaican birds on a tree by the beach stretched his wings and then launched himself into the clear sky. I followed his progress until I once more lost myself in my thoughts. When I looked again the bird was just a dot in the distance. It reminded me of watching the homing pigeons as a child. They would fly bravely to their destination and I would send my thoughts with them – perhaps they were on their outward trip to some faraway destination or just heading home.

The Bob Marley song finished and I smiled again as I remembered how much I liked him when I was a child. The pain of being teased and laughed at by the other kids in school had now gone. Once I would crawl reluctantly from one day to the next. Now I couldn't wait to get up every morning and make the most of all the time I had, even if I needed to do nothing more than be with my family. Perhaps I would take a stroll down to the local market and buy a Bob Marley T-shirt that said, 'Could You Be Loved'…